Maya Phillips is a certified NLP practitioner and holds a diploma in Ericsonian Hypnosis and Counseling. She is a pioneer in the field of 'Emotional Medicine' and the use of autogenic Metaphor and Archetypes in problem solving and therapy. As a teacher in the field of human consciousness, she combines an innovative psycho-spiritual perspective with insight into the emotional, physical and spiritual aspects of problems. She specializes in facilitating others to discover and realize their inborn emotional intelligence, increase their capacity for loving and develop spiritual gifts.

In 1994, Maya Phillips developed the therapeutic system of Emotional Mapping which teaches people how to discover, explore and resolve life issues by interacting with and testing their unique and personal inner metaphors and archetypes. This method was first outlined in *The A to Z of Life Maintenance* which she co-authored with Max Comfort.

by the same author

The A to Zen of Life Maintenance
(co-authored with Max Comfort)

Emotional Excellence

A PRACTICAL GUIDE TO SELF-DISCOVERY

Maya Phillips

ELEMENT

Shaftesbury, Dorset • Boston, Massachusetts
Melbourne, Victoria

© Element Books Limited 1997
Text, Emotional Maps and Body Charts © Maya Phillips 1997

Emotional Mapping, Multi Level Reading and Metascape are
registered trademarks.

First published in the UK in 1997 by
Elements Books Limited

This paperback edition first
published in the UK in 1999 by
Element Books Limited
Shaftesbury, Dorset SP7 8BP

Published in the USA in 1999 by
Element Books, Inc.
160 North Washington Street
Boston, MA 02114

Published in Australia in 1999 by
Element Books and distributed
by Penguin Books Australia Limited
487 Maroondah Highway, Ringwood,
Victoria 3134

Cover design by The Design Revolution, Brighton
Text design by Roger Lightfoot
Typeset by Footnote Graphics, Warminster, Wilts
Printed and bound in Great Britain by Creative Print and Design (Wales),
Ebbw Vale

British Library Cataloguing in Publication
data available

Library of Congress Cataloging in Publication
data available

ISBN 1 86204 374 4

Contents

Acknowledgements

This book is dedicated to those who, while no longer here in body, will always be with me in spirit:

To my grandma Jane Phillips. Your absolute love and friendship have had a tremendous and lasting influence on my life. Your gentle, ever caring presence and generous disposition will guide me always. Thank you.

Dad, I know you often felt that life dealt you the joker in the pack. In this game the joker is wild. It can be anything you need it to be. Wherever you find yourself, wherever your spirit takes you, remember that laughter and music are the best healing medicine. Rest in peace. I love you.

To my sister Vanessa. Somewhere in the heavens the light of your smile still shines. You are in my heart and in my thoughts. I miss you.

To my wonderful friends. As I write I am reminded of the abundance of love, support, encouragement and caring that exists in my life . . .

Vikky, I am so aware of the hours that you spent typing up and organizing my original hand-written text; for the laborious effort you put into the illustrations and for the caring encouragement that you always offer me. Really, I couldn't have done this without you.

Poppy, Charlie, Thea, Harriet and others who contributed their time and Emotional Maps to this book. I trust that your healing processes will inspire others.

My son Daniel who knows how to share the best kind of hugs. You still make and serve the finest cup of tea I have ever tasted. I am always encouraged by your enthusiasm, love and thoughtfulness.

Jazz, to whom the words commitment and freedom are synonymous. Your talents and attributes are too numerous to mention. I appreciate all the time, technical expertise and love that you have invested in me.

Introduction

WHAT'S THIS ALL ABOUT ANYWAY?

This book is about the use and abuse of emotion. It is a course in emotional mastery. I am going to share with you my experience as an emotional trainer and tour guide. Over the years I have helped numerous individuals develop from emotional couch potatoes into people with great emotional strength and flexibility. I have been privileged to be a witness for those who have been working on the Emotional Excellence programme. My friends and students (and I have to include myself) have examined areas of our lives which we felt would benefit from some improvement. The Emotional Excellence programme showed us how to examine and observe ourselves without discrimination or rationale. This has led each of us to experience a level of self-respect and inner trust that we had not encountered before. Life has taken on a new perspective. I find myself surrounded by self-confident, emotionally proficient people, who respond to the challenges of life in a proactive and self-actualizing way. Without exception every participant has reached a new level of health, wealth and happiness.

I believe this programme can do the same for you

You have a built-in aptitude toward learning. It is something you do all the time; it cannot be avoided and it often happens out of your conscious awareness. This programme utilizes your natural ability to its greatest capacity. All the exercises are designed to incite both the conscious and non-conscious aspects of your bodymind. From the moment you begin the course you will discover how to bypass any unnecessary chatter in your head. You will develop a stronger relationship with your body and recognize how it influences your thoughts. Mind and body are so bound together that in order to remind myself of the inextricable connection I like to refer to it as the bodymind. Relaxation and reading exercises help you to change the patterns of your brain waves from the 'wide awake' delta state to the 'resting' alpha state and the 'super resting' theta state. During periods of alpha and theta brain states the different functions of your brain become increasingly synchronized. The effect is an increased ability to relax, focus and feel centred. Your aptitude for learning and memorizing information increases dramatically and you will be able to make any desired changes to your behaviour and your life easily and without force. Furthermore, to encourage completion of each task, all exercises in Part 1 lead to feelings of relaxation and pleasure. I am certain that you will discover a new level of curiosity that will encourage you to continue your journey toward self-discovery.

When driving a car you are doing several things at once. For instance, you have a destination in mind and at the same time you are following a route while being simultaneously aware of other traffic and making decisions about speed. Whilst your attention is focused on the road ahead your arms, feet and legs automatically coordinate to drive the car. You are being multi-tasked. What do you think would happen if you had to think about all these actions at once? To keep you safe some of your actions have to be automatic. Your conscious and non-conscious mind become synchronized and technically speaking you are in a trance.

Emotional Excellence makes use of this natural phenomenon to help the reader recall events, access hidden information and enhance learning. While on this course you will be asked many questions. You will find that the answers are readily available. They come from within you. As all your discoveries are self-motivated it is easy for you to take the information on board. Thus changes in perspective, understanding and behaviour are inevitable.

People are complex organisms. Science is beginning to

recognize through the study of consciousness that we are more than our bodies; there is some suggestion that we may even be more than our minds. Emotional Excellence simultaneously develops your awareness of your body-mind, emotions and your spirit (I think of this as the essence of your non-physical self). The experience is rather like meeting old friends after a long absence and getting to know them again. As these friendships mature, where there had been internal conflict you will begin to notice continuity and cooperation. You will naturally begin to realize your true potential in ways that you could not have imagined.

Our fantasies are stepping stones to our reality

When you start a physical training regime you expect to find muscles that you did not realize you had. If you work too hard or fast, do not learn to use the gym equipment and do not listen to your instructor you can often impede your progress. If you wish to gain the best result from this course, it is important that you start gently, follow the instructions and complete the exercises in the order that they are presented. Please use my knowledge as it will stand you in good stead throughout.

We are used to reading a book from beginning to end, picking it up as we fancy and putting it down again when our need has been satisfied. This, however, is more than just a book: it is a dynamic home study course of which you the reader are an integral part. This is a powerful learning programme. To achieve thorough and lasting results you will need to work with the contents in a manner that may at first seem to be unusual or even unnecessary. Some of the chapters and exercises will be very easy to absorb while others will need to be re-read and practised before you can comfortably move on. There will also be times when you will not be able to read at all. This experience occurs when you are inwardly processing or integrating any new learning.

Your experience of reading this book will be different to that of anyone else because you are an active component in the learning process. Therefore you are likely to find that the relationship that you develop with the book, itself dictates the speed at which you can work with and complete it.

> *Readers are of two sorts: those who carefully go through a book and those who carefully let the book go through them*

Consider this book to be a travelling companion, a workbook and an encyclopaedia. It is full of ideas, facts, thoughts, feelings, beliefs, images, half-truths, perceptions, honesty, laughter, inspiration, love and, of course, emotion. It will all at once ebb and flow, freeze and thaw and gently melt away your self-doubt and your fear, until you too are encouraged to master the power of Emotional Excellence.

WHY DID I WRITE THIS BOOK?

Like most of you who are reading this book, I was brought up in a Western society. This is a culture of acquisition – filled with opportunities for those with an education, or for those who dare, but it is also a culture that teaches us to consider feelings as indulgence or irrelevant nonsense. So ingrained is this thinking that we relegate emotion to the periphery of our lives and place a high value on the suppression of our emotions. We 'grin and bare it', 'pull ourselves together', 'keep a stiff upper lip' and 'just get on with it' to such a degree that our emotion has no other option but to make itself known to us in a very powerful and distorted form. Through suppression, misunderstanding and neglect, emotion can be seen expressed in an exaggerated form throughout society. Look at the epidemic proportions of the rave culture with its widespread and respected drug use. Violence on the football terraces, road rage, territorial gang wars, battered wives, abused and neglected children, stress-related accidents, injury and illnesses – these become the accepted face of modern society, and the list of personal self-inflicted abuse goes on and on. We are all to one degree or another swimming against this tide of un-expressed feeling. It distorts our lives and warps our potential. In an attempt to regain control we become more insular and self-protective, less caring and less civilized.

This book is a plea for the return of sanity. It is an attempt to reintroduce individuals to that neglected side of their nature so that emotion, rather than being seen as a mystery – or the evil contents of a Pandora's Box, that once released will never return to the confines of the container – can be experienced as a liberating and creative force which directs us towards fulfilling our true potential in a self-nurturing and self-respectful way. Through choosing to find the best in ourselves we can be open to nurturing and accepting the best in others. And I wonder what would happen if we all did that?

HOW TO MAKE THE MOST OF THIS BOOK

This book is presented in 5 parts, 1 to 5. Each part is designed to initiate, facilitate and develop specific 'emotional muscles' and particular emotional mastery techniques:

Part 1 aims to show you how to relax mind and body to create a synergy, literally a synthesis of energy, between the two. This is achieved through breathing techniques, relaxation, visualization and 'multi-level reading'.

Part 2 develops the theme of bodymind synergy through the use of specific exercises. It also introduces the concept of metaphor as the language of emotion and shows how an intention can (and usually does) influence outcome.

Part 3 introduces Emotional Mapping.™

Part 4 explains self-esteem and self-value through the techniques and methods from previous chapters.

Part 5 addresses goal achievement, motivation and commitment.

Each module is subdivided into chapters. Within each chapter there will be lessons. The lessons are designed to help you learn about yourself. (Remember the outcome here is self-mastery.) By reading, you will be given three opportunities to discover, or rediscover, something that will benefit you.

The 1st opportunity presents itself as a thought-provoking conversation based on a theme such as relaxation or thinking. At this point I would like to say that I am not attempting to indoctrinate you. I do not insist that I am right, or wrong for that matter, I am simply creating a space in which you can have the room, and time, to consider your opinions and perspective. What you conclude is up to you.

The 2nd opportunity will be a practical task such as mind clearing, relaxation training or answering questions about yourself. Writing exercises will be marked by a symbol like this: ✍. You will need a note pad, sketch book, coloured pens and something to write with for these sections. You may expect to be informed, challenged, amused and illuminated!

The 3rd opportunity comes in the form of an innovative reading exercise which we call 'multi-level reading'. This will be indicated by a symbol like this: ◗ . These exercises are written in such a way as to communicate directly with your unconscious mind whilst simultaneously building a bridge between the different areas and functions of your brain. The writing style induces a deep learning state that leads on to an attitude of self-cooperation. While in this frame of mind, your mind and body can synchronize and areas of physical, mental and emotional concern are effortlessly addressed. Quite simply through the action of reading you will bring about positive physical, psychological, biochemical and emotional change. Rather like a fingerprint, these changes will be peculiar to you and specifically for your own benefit. Multi-level reading has been tried and tested: 'It really is a completely effortless way of learning and gaining insight about yourself', said one client. 'It has a power-fully relaxing effect on me which increases my ability to absorb and integrate what I have read, and influences my capacity for visualization and realization.'

As you progress through the training, clients and volunteers have reported that you can expect to achieve immediate benefits in the following:

- Relaxation and stress management skills
- Greater body awareness
- Increased physical and mental balance
- Rapid and creative thinking
- Confident self-expression
- Accelerated learning ability
- Good memory recall
- Stronger logic and intuitive ability
- Successful problem solving skills
- Emotional honesty
- Rapid healing ability
- Effective communication
- Strong supportive relationships
- Increased self-confidence and self-awareness
- Rapid and effective decision making
- Deeper spiritual connection
- Increase in psychic awareness and ability
- Emotional Mapping
- Self-trust
- Self-respect and responsibility
- The ability to create a successful future

So what are we waiting for? Turn the page and lets get started . . .

Whatever you can do, or dream you can, begin it. Boldness has genius, power and magic in it.

Goethe

Part 1

1 Basic training

Before we go any further you are going to need some basic equipment. This will include:

- A lined pad – preferably one you find attractive both to touch and to look at
- A plain pad
- Coloured pens and crayons
- Something to write with
- A comfy chair – make sure you can place both feet flat on the floor

Or

- A favourite piece of floor – with a wall on which to rest your back
- Cushions
- A rug or blanket
- Some uninterrupted time – set your answerphone and switch off the phone, please

Several of the exercises in this book will be more effective when you experience them with closed eyes. Unless you have an extraordinary memory you will need hi-fi equipment on which you can play tapes and record voices. They are marked with a tape symbol: ⊙⊙ . Recording them is also time saving as you are going to be repeating them often. As you become accustomed to the training programme you can practise anywhere. Many students take themselves into nature, a train on the subway, during a workbreak, and one or two even practise in the bath!

If you don't have a tape recorder ask a friend to read through the exercises with you. On this occasion two is definitely company and three or more becomes a work group.

You are about to 'Prime Your Mind'. This is the equivalent of stretching before a physical workout. It will help to release bodymind tension and give you high-quality fuel – oxygen to be precise. Read the exercise all the way through before you begin. It is in three parts. Follow the instructions and then take it slowly.

1. Stand with your feet slightly apart – make sure they are parallel
Unlock (relax) your knees
Take a deep breath, fill your lungs
Blow out hard enough to make a good noise
Repeat this three times

2. Hold your position
As you breathe in deeply lift your right arm
Hold this pose for a slow count of four
Breathe out slowly and return your arm to a resting position
Repeat this breathing stretch with the left arm
Good. Now repeat the total movement three times for each side of your body

3. Breathing Numbers

This is a basic relaxation exercise which reduces the effects of stress. As tension is released you will find that blood will circulate more freely to your muscles. This may result in sensations of warmth, coolness, or tingling in certain parts of the body. This is natural and means you are getting a result.

Find somewhere comfortable to sit
Close your eyes and simply breathe slowly to a count of four
Draw the breath in 1 2 3 4, and gently sigh it out 1 2 3 4
Breathe deeply in 1 2 3 4, and relax it out 1 2 3 4
Deeply in 2 3 4, relax out 2 3 4
Deeply in 2 3 4, relax out 2 3 4
Deeply in 2 3 4, relax out 2 3 4
Good. Draw the breath in, relax the breath out
That's it, just breathe in (pause 2 3 4) and out (pause 2 3 4)
Again (pause for a count of 7)

Just keep breathing and as you do so you will find yourself noticing how tension moves out of your body with each exhalation. Begin to pay attention to the movement of your breath in and out. Allow your breath to even out at a level that is perfect for you. Just sit (pause for a count of 4), observe your breath (pause for the count of 8), let your breath enliven and relax your body as you sit. You only need your breath and a heartbeat to refresh and unwind. That's really fine (pause for 4) a breath and a heartbeat. Become familiar with the feeling. How comfortable can your body become? You can continue to breathe and find out. (Pause now for 30 seconds.) Whenever you need to feel refreshed you can now unwind as you sit and pay attention to your self and your body. Pay attention to yourself right now, breathe, recognize how and where you feel sensations in your body. (Pause for 15 seconds.) That's fine, thank you; you are doing great. Just know that whatever you are experiencing is absolutely right for you at this moment in time, and that your experience may change every time you choose to relax and unwind.

Now take a very deep breath, sigh the breath out hard. (Pause.) That's it. And again, take a very deep breath, blow out hard. Good. Take a very deep breath and then blow out hard. Now breathe in. Stretch your arms and shoulders.

Open your eyes, breathe out. How much better do you feel now?

Well done, that completes the first part of your basic training. That was your first lesson in being constructively still. You will be repeating this exercise in many different forms throughout this book. Remember that whatever happened is absolutely appropriate. There are no rights or wrongs. This is your first lesson and we are not looking for perfection. Come to think of it we never look for perfection, we just trust that you will be inspired by your results to develop your own level of excellence at whatever pace suits you. Now just to reassure you that you are doing fine, here is a list of what other people have experienced whilst doing the exercise:

- Slower breathing
- More relaxed body
- Sharper hearing – external sounds may become heightened, but don't necessarily bother you
- Chilliness
- A slight feeling of tiredness
- Twitching muscles
- Numbness in hands or feet
- Heavier or lighter body sensations
- Rumbling stomach
- Heavy or flickering eyelids
- Awareness of your own breathing

Now take a 10-minute break, have something to drink and come back to us, OK?

Aim for success not perfection.
Never give up your right to be wrong
because then you will loose the ability to
learn new things and move forward in life.
Dr David M. Burns

2 A bit more basic

What gives you pleasure?

What was the *first* thought that came to mind?

Write it down in your notebook right now.

That is a good start. Now just keep on thinking about what gives you pleasure, what makes you feel good, and how much fun you can have.

Just to inspire you and help you jog your memory here are some memories I came up with whilst writing this chapter.

The first blossom in spring. Meditating out in the open. Listening to my kitten purring while she sleeps on my chest. Playing in the ocean with my son. Working with like-minded people. Watching other people strive and succeed. Sucking iced coffee through a straw. Licking Ho Sin sauce off my fingers. Growing fruit and vegetables. The feeling you get when you first fall in love. The feeling you get when you remember why you fell in love. Music, music, music. Open air theatre. *Star Trek* . . .

The list could go on and on and in fact it did. The very first time I did that exercise I ended up with 359 things on my list and a grin as big as a Cheshire cat. The grin lasted for several days because I just kept remembering things that made me feel good. Now whenever life gets too challenging I make a 'happy list'.

OK, now it's your turn. Write or doodle your thoughts right now. Get those images down on paper. Think happy. Think something wonderful. Don't be concerned if you can't think of anything or only one or two ideas come to mind. We all have off days on occasion. Go back to the list above. It may jog your memory. Read each item in turn; you could rediscover your own inspiration. Take as long as you need and come back to the book later.

Welcome back. How do you feel now? Yes, you can add that to your happy list too if you like! Take a few moments to do a quick body scan and check how thinking wonderful, happy, pleasurable thoughts makes your body feel. Just pay attention to your body by focusing on your head and moving that focus all the way down to your feet. Isn't it interesting to discover that thinking good makes you feel good, and when you feel good you naturally relax. Relaxation is like any other skill, the more you practise the easier it gets. What's more, the results are cumulative, so the benefits are greater with time. To test the effectiveness, you can repeat your basic relaxation exercise now. It is repeated below.

[◎◎]

Set your answerphone and switch off the phone please
Find somewhere comfortable to sit
Close your eyes and simply breathe slowly to a count of four
Draw the breath in 1 2 3 4, and gently sigh it out 1 2 3 4
Breathe deeply in 1 2 3 4, and relax it out 1 2 3 4
Deeply in 2 3 4, relax out 2 3 4
Deeply in 2 3 4, relax out 2 3 4
Deeply in 2 3 4, relax out 2 3 4
Good. Draw the breath in, relax the breath out
That's it. Just breathe in (pause 2 3 4) and out (pause 2 3 4)
Again (pause for a count of 7)

Just keep breathing and as you do so find yourself noticing how tension moves out of your body with each exhalation. Begin to pay attention to the movement of your breath in and out. Allow your breath to even out at a level that is perfect for you. Just sit (pause for a count of 4), observe your breath (pause for the count of 8), let your breath enliven and relax your body as you sit. You only need your breath and a heartbeat to refresh and unwind. That's really fine (pause for 4) – a breath and a heartbeat. Become familiar with the feeling. How comfortable can your body become? You can continue to breathe and find out. (Pause now for 30 seconds.) Whenever you need to feel refreshed you can now unwind as you sit and pay attention to your self and your body. Pay attention to yourself right now, breathe, recognize how and where you feel sensations in your body. (Pause for 15 seconds.) That's fine, thank you; you are doing great. Just know that whatever you are experiencing is absolutely right for you at this moment in time, and that your experience may change every time you choose to relax and unwind.

Now take a very deep breath, sigh the breath out hard (pause)
Again, take a very deep breath, blow out hard. You have done this before and it was fun
Take a very deep breath and then blow out hard

Breathe in. Stretch your arms and shoulders
Open your eyes, breathe out. How much better do you feel now?

Take the time to record your experience in your notebook
Remember to note how you feel physically, emotionally and mentally

3 Here's another fine mess you've got me into

As a therapist I have noticed it is not only my clients who experience struggle and confusion. For each of us there is usually some area of life that just doesn't work out, no matter how hard we try to make changes. You know about problems. We all have our fair share. Yours are personal to you. If you are anything like the people I meet, you probably spend a lot of time talking about them and trying to find solutions. Everyone I come across has something to gripe about and we all have strong feelings and ideas about how life should be and what it would look like if only the problems would go away.

Have you noticed what happens when you try to push your nagging emotions to one side? Do you attempt to avoid confrontation and find yourself pushing the troublesome areas of your life under the carpet? That's like ignoring the woodworm under the rug. Like unresolved problems, those little grubs eat silently away the wooden boards until one day you step on the weak spot, lose your footing and fall through the floor. Do you get the picture? What you haven't realized yet is that much of that pain and suffering is quite unnecessary. You have not recognized that you often spend time focusing attention on the pain and bewilderment instead of focusing attention on a way of making a difference.

Making a difference means addressing your difficulties and fears from the wisdom and strength that lies within you. It is the action of intentionally shifting your attention from your emotional couch potato towards the developing skill and flexibility of your emotional athlete. Just look toward your successes and victories.

They did not just happen; no one was there waving a magic wand over your head. You took certain actions and they created a positive result. If you can do it once you can do it again.

If you do not feel wise or strong right now do not despair. I believe that you have all the knowledge and resources that you need to make that difference. They may not be all that obvious to you just yet but just as a gemmologist can tell a rough diamond from a pebble, I have been privileged to see the gems and riches of everyone I meet, however well disguised.

Making a difference is not necessarily the same thing as finding a solution to what ails you right now; it does not always create an instant result, but the result will be timed to perfection, exactly what you need and the benefits will be long-lasting.

I trust absolutely that somewhere inside you, you know all the answers and you have the desire to find them even if you don't know how to access them yet – why else would you have bought this book? Surely not as an ornament to adorn your shelf, or as a wedge to prop up your table leg. Owning this book is not enough: you will have to read it thoroughly. You will need to continue the journey and invest time and energy in completing the exercises and experimenting with the techniques in order to reach the rich rewards.

4   *Emotion is energy*

When thinking EMOTION think movement, think water. Play with the word.

E M O T I O N – MOTION – OTION(ocean) – ION(eon) – MOTE(moat) – EMOTE(feel)

How many words and meanings are contained within that one small word? What do they mean for you? What do you think and feel and see? How do they have meaning?

Emotion should not be still; it is movement. It can be used or abused, your best friend or a prison out of which you view the world. It is about those sensations and images that flow through your mind and body that help you to make sense of your world. It is about how you choose or do not choose to interpret that flow. Why is all this important anyway?

Are you a raging torrent, sweeping everything up in its path?
A tiny trickle of a stream soaking into the earth and making it fertile?
A pond filled with life bursting bubbles on your surface, deep and green
and cool?
Are you inviting?
Where is your stagnant water, dark, unfragrant, breeding flies?
What pests!

At any given moment in time you are all and none of these. Feelings are not always recognizable. Like thoughts they are random. They are not neatly edited lines of text or carefully edited celluloid frames. They are complex, rich and diverse. It is your will, your ability to focus, the time you spend attending to each notion that will determine where you are on your life path and where you can go next.

Whatever your current position, through this book you gain the desire to travel. You will begin an epic journey into the centre of yourself. This book will be your guide. We will spend time exploring your inner terrain together, and you will find the time and the confidence to explore alone. You will discover your most ambitious dreams. Perhaps you will find some hidden places of wonder. There may be nooks and crannies where secrets lie like seeds, some frozen in time, dormant, waiting for the right time and condition to burst into life. You may find dams and dry river beds or marsh choking with weeds in need of draining. Wherever you find yourself you will be gaining knowledge of your true potential and building the tools to help you get there.

Here is another of those tools. This tool will bring into focus even the most active mind and help you to develop your bodymind connection. To get the best from this exercise you will need to read through it first. Then either get a friend to read it for you as you sit comfortably with your eyes closed, or record it yourself and play it back later. You will need:

A comfy chair – make sure you can place both feet flat on the floor

Or

A favourite piece of floor – with a wall on which to rest your back
Cushions
A rug or blanket – your body may cool down as you become more
rested
Some uninterrupted time – set your answerphone and switch off the
phone please

Sit comfortably with both feet flat on the floor, your back
supported and as straight as possible. Place your hands loosely in
your lap. As you close your eyes take a deep breath, and relax the
breath out. (pause) Again take a deep breath and relax the breath
out. (pause) And once more. Take a deep breath and relax the
breath out. Good. Focus your attention on your face. Remember
your basic training. Breathe in 2, 3, 4 and out 2, 3, 4, and in 2, 3,
4 and out 2, 3, 4. While thinking 'face' breathe in deeply, slowly
to the count of four. Good. Now your whole head. Breathe
deeply. Focus your attention on your head. That's it, draw the
breath in, relax the breath out. Know that each breath in brings
energy and oxygen into your body and each breath out releases
toxins and tension. (pause) Each breath in brings energy and
oxygen into your body and each breath out releases toxins and
tension. (pause) OK. Continue to breathe to the count of four
and as you breathe listen to the instructions. Focus your
attention on your chest. Breathe deeply, in 2, 3, 4 and out 2, 3, 4
and breathe as you focus now on your upper back and shoulders.
Know that each breath in brings energy and oxygen into your
body and each breath out releases toxins and tension. (pause)
That's good, now abdomen and lower back. In - - - and out - - -
That's right. Each time you breathe you can become aware of the
changing sensations within your body. Breathe into your arms
now. Remember energy and oxygen releases tension and toxins.
In - - - and out - - - What are the changing sensations in that part
of your body? Where is the movement in you? (pause) Focus on
your legs, thighs, breathe in - - - and out - - - and calves. That's

good. Now your feet and hands. Energy in - - - tensions out - - - Each time you breathe you will notice comfortable sensations moving throughout your body. Just continue breathing and recall your 'happy list' as energy fills your body and you can release tension with each outward breath. When you feel good you think good. How good can breathing make you feel? (pause) Now breathe normally, just allow your body to find the right depth of breath for you. (pause) That's right, it is no effort at all, to notice how your body feels when you think happy wonderful thoughts. (pause) Notice the most pleasurable sensation in your body right now. (pause) What do you notice? Where is your attention focused at this moment? (pause) Now as you breathe shift your attention (pause) move the focus to another part of your body. (pause) How has the sensation moved with your thought? (pause) Breathe, and know that energy moves to your point of focus. You may notice some pleasurable sensation moving to this part of your body as energy follows your thought. Where are you focused now? (pause) How good does that feel? (pause) As you think happy thoughts, how much better does the feeling get with each breath? (pause to the count of 10) Isn't it interesting to realize that you can change the way your body feels simply by closing your eyes and focusing attention upon happy thoughts as you breathe rhythmically.

Be still now and focus on your feet. You can feel the floor beneath your feet. Focus on your feet. (speaking slightly louder and faster) Now focus on your feet and as you feel your feet flex and wiggle your toes. Stretch your body. Breathe in deeply and blow out hard. And again breathe deeply in and blow out hard. Be ready to *stretch your body and open your eyes.* Look around you. What colours can you see? That was an interesting exercise. Well done.

Make a note of everything you can remember – take all the time you need. It will be useful later.

If you would like to achieve more rapid and permanent results with this programme, tape the above exercise speaking clearly, slowly and melodiously. Listen to it each night before sleeping for at least two weeks. Thereafter listen to it once a week or as you feel the need.

This exercise has been tried and tested many times over. To reassure you that your responses are quite normal here are some examples from past students of the things we would have expected you to notice:

- 'I was able to spot where I held tension'
- 'I got a bit dizzy'
- 'I felt light-headed and had to stop'
- 'I felt more steady and balanced afterwards'
- 'I had feelings of being much more relaxed, focused and composed'
- 'I was able to dissolve my tension away just through breathing'
- 'I actually experienced the sensation of tension moving out of my shoulders and down through my feet'
- 'My tension became almost tangible – that was scary'
- 'I had been sluggish for days, now I feel better'
- 'It was hard at first, but with practice I'm feeling the benefit'
- 'After doing this for several days in a row my outlook has been much more positive and I feel more active'

If you can't sit still, can't concentrate, or you become irritated or feel inconvenienced, you may be rather tired or stressed out. Go back to your taped basic breathing exercise in Chapter 1. Get some rest and do this again later.

Now take a short break and then do something completely different.

5 *Influential reading*

Those of you who completed the last exercise will have already experienced a huge benefit. Well done. For the rest of my readers, I understand that there are a lot of demands on your time and life can be very challenging. I empathize with your plight. I also realize that when asked to stop everything to do an exercise, it can seem easier to just keep right on reading. To resolve the conflict between making the most of yourself and getting everything else done, this book is about to help you to fulfil more of your bodymind potential.

You are about to add another dimension to your learning ability simply by reading. We learn all the time whether we realize it or not. Sometimes that learning is easy and enjoyable. At other times the lessons can be hard or difficult and we may think them inappropriate or of no consequence. How many times have you heard the statement, 'If I had known such and such I would have handled it totally differently'? Often you do not have all the information you need in order to make sense of whatever it is that's going on. Under these circumstances you can become confused, dismissive or defensive and your ability to learn easily is hampered. Have you ever wondered why small children learn so quickly? Watch them play. They are interested in everything. They explore, fiddle, taste, touch and smell anything they come across. When you have an inquiring mind you will automatically approach any situation with a sense of curiosity. Any sense of confusion and resistance almost magically evaporates into thin air as you discover something new and surprising from every event. Thus, whatever the outcome your time will have been productive and well spent.

One of the ways that we learn is from books. Pages and pages of words strung together in a specific order designed to impart information of one kind or another. A good book, one that you enjoy, fires your imagination. With a novel you may have a strong impression of the characters and their whereabouts. Perhaps you even develop an emotional connection or relate to their lives in some way? Some books are more influential than others. Consider the impact of the Bible, the Koran, the Torah and other religious and spiritual writing. What about political literature? It is easy to see the kind of influence and impact that global leaders have had on society, both for good and bad.

As you continue to read this book you may wonder what the benefit or influence can be. This is where curiosity can be a wonderful asset. It can allow you to speculate about an outcome. When you question you become open and receptive to the possibility that you can gain far more than you can envisage.

It is now time to discover something about yourself that you had not recognized yet. I have absolutely no idea what that may be because I do not know you. However, I do know this book. It is designed to bring out the best in you, so be assured that you are going to find something positive. As you practise Multi Level Reading℠, the 'something positive' will be coaxed gently into your conscious awareness from your unconscious mind. It will be specific to you and it will be something that you can benefit from right now. (All Multi Level Reading exercises are indicated by this symbol and a change in the style of font.)

Christopher Robin came down from the forest to the bridge, feeling all sunny and careless, and just as if twice nineteen didn't matter a bit, as it didn't on such a happy afternoon, and he thought that if he stood on the bottom rail of the bridge, and leant over, and watched the river slipping slowly away beneath him, then he would suddenly know everything that there was to be known, and he would be able to tell Pooh, who wasn't quite sure

about some of it. But when he got to the bridge and saw all the animals there, then he knew that it wasn't that kind of afternoon, but the other kind, when you wanted to do something.

Read the paragraphs below slowly and carefully. Pause momentarily at each full stop. A gap of about one second is ideal but you will develop your own reading pace with practice. Some people have found it useful to multi-level read to soothing or relaxing music. Classical music like Mozart, Beethoven and Bach is known to be popular.

As you look down at this page and re-focus on these words you may ascertain that it is easy to discover more about yourself as you read. You cannot help but recognize the words on the page as you take the weight of this book in your hands. How does this book feel to your fingers as you hold it? As you read the text where do you notice the most pressure? Is it on the palm of one hand or on the other? How do your fingertips notice the weight of these type-filled pages? And as you begin to realize exactly how you hold this book you may also recognize that you are making some adjustments with your hands and fingers. Could you hold this book more comfortably or is it fine just as it is?

Life is so very full of questions and there are very many questions that you will ask and answer while reading these pages. I wonder what you will discover before this passage ends? How curious can you be about what you can find out as your eyes skim across this page? Can you recall breathing to the count of four? What happens to your chest as you remember? What kind of breathing have you practised in this way as you read this book? How do you breathe in that way now? Isn't it interesting to discover that you can re-create an experience just by re-membering it? So, as you remember these things, your eyes can follow these words as you discover in your own particular way, that an experience you have had before can be even better now. Now you know you can notice the pace of your breathing. What is it that you notice as you become more and more aware of the pace of your breathing? By paying attention you may discover something that you had not noticed yet. I wonder what that might be?

Perhaps you can notice how your thoughts can be here and somewhere else at the same time? How is it that a pleasurable thought can enter your mind whilst you sit and read and wonder what you can discover? How do you detect a thought in your mind? Could it be an image? Is there some other way you can tell? Have you noticed yet that your thoughts can seem to flow from one place to another? Have you noticed that every thought you have can create some image or feeling or sound or something specific to you? You know that sometimes a thought can be a memory. Some memories are so much fun to remember, aren't they? What fun can you recall now? And how can that memory feel better and better as you read on? As you find out, your mind may wander as you find that pleasing memory again and again.

Now I do not know what you can see in your mind, but I do know that you can recognize that you can be in this room reading this material, and at the same time be in your own world of image and sound. So simply by running your eyes over the typeface in front of you, and recalling things in your own special way, you can tap into the vast resource of memory and experience in your mind. Your mind is a powerful tool. It can, as you read, recall all the information you need to be aware of now. As it recalls something positive it can exclude information that you do not need to be aware of right now. It is so effortless to read now, and later when you need to remember more how surprised you can be to know that you can recall all the information you need so easily. I wonder how your mind can do it? You know you already know so much – nevertheless you can discover more. What would you like to know? When will you know that you know it?

I know that you have an awareness that time can seem to stretch and shrink. It always speeds by when you are having fun and time was well spent. Now listen for your breath once more. How does your chest rise and fall as you breathe in and out? Now I am aware that some change has occurred. I do not know for sure what changes you will notice, but I know that you can notice that, amongst other things, there is a change in your level of relaxation. As you continue to notice these things you may begin to wonder how reading this text can develop your learning ability. And only you can find out. So, as you develop the ability to observe and appreciate these changes you can be as surprised as you like to discover that there are so many different ways to find out. Now as you breathe you can inhale more deeply and draw that knowledge into conscious awareness so that you can discover the many benefits in your own way.

As this passage comes to a close you will begin to refocus all your attention on the text right now. The words will somehow be clearer and sharper to your eyes as you listen to the words you read. Once again find yourself present here. You can be more aware of your body now. How does it feel to have your feet resting on the floor? As you finish this sentence you can become absolutely wide awake. Alert and focused in the present now. Ready to stretch and stand and walk around.

During the last exercise you will have entered into an *altered world*. This world will often exclude some awareness of your present reality. Thus you are in an *altered state*. Throughout this book many of the exercises will be presented in the form of Multi Level Reading exercises much like the one you have just experienced. During workshops and sessions people have commented that the initial results can seem very subtle. It seems that the effect of Multi Level Reading is cumulative. However the overall results will be powerful and profound.

One client said, 'This really is a completely effortless way of learning. In each exercise your mind focuses on and integrates something new. Sometimes I found my thoughts drifting, at other times I was aware of my mind performing three or four different functions simultaneously. Just by reading I have gained insight into my unconscious and have actually felt shifts and changes occur, giving rise to realizations about my self.'

Multi Level Reading seems to work by accessing directly your unconscious mind. Your unconscious mind then goes about answering or seeking answers to the questions you are asked, and checking and verifying the statements that are made during the exercise. The exercises are designed to be instructive rather than directive. This allows your mind the freedom to pick and choose what information is appropriate for you. No two people ever experience exactly the same results. Through Multi Level Reading you will have the opportunity to practise learning in a whole brain-altered state. As you learn in this way you are utilizing more of your brain's considerable potential than if you were simply reading normally. You will soon be discovering the benefits of using your brain in a whole new way. You will instinctively know how to change your mind for your highest benefit and how to develop your imagination as a tool for success.

To the untrained mind the world seems dull
To the illuminated mind the whole universe gleams and sparkles
with colour and light

6 *There is some wisdom in everything*

In order to achieve healing, which in this book really means experiencing a state of self-containment and the desire and ability to express and receive love, we must first be ready to recognize that we are starting from a place of damage. As a therapist I have come to understand that when clients tell you their story or ask you to help them achieve their goal, they are talking to you from their damage, from pain and from a twisted or unbalanced perspective.

We all carry some kind of pain or anger. How do your problems make themselves known to you? They may look or feel like physical or mental illness, insomnia, poverty or debt, lack of confidence, overeating or substance abuse, poor relationships or a habit you may want to break. With new understanding, some training and lots of application you can transform your current situation and make that difference we talked about earlier.

Life is full of metaphors. We use them to help us understand something new. In the same way when attempting to make sense of our lives we often make links with the past in order to make sense of the present. So what has life taught you? What do you believe about yourself, the world and the people in it?

> *Life is what happens while you're busy making other plans*
> John Lennon

> *Nobody, as long as he moves about among the chaotic currents of life is without trouble*
>
> Carl Jung

Life is like a box of chocolates, you never know what you're gonna get.

Forrest Gump

Life's a gas!
Marc Bolan

You must see the world as a wonderful place before it can be one.
Richard Wilkins

Life is no brief candle to me. It is a sort of splendid torch which I've got to hold up for the moment and I want to make it burn as brightly as possible before handing it on to future generations.
George Bernard Shaw

If you're alive you gotta jump around a lot because, as I see it, life is the very opposite of death, so if you're quiet, you're not living. You've got to be noisy, or at least your thoughts should be noisy and colourful and lively.

Mel Brooks

Life is an onion: you peel it off one layer at a time and sometimes you weep.

Carl Sandburg

Life was never meant to be a struggle.
Stuart Wilde

Life is a play. It's not its length but its performance that counts.
Seneca

Life's a bitch! Life's a beach! Life is hard and then you die. Life is a cabaret! Life is a rollercoaster ride. Life's a bowl of cherries! Life is sacred.

It is the messages that lie within your mind and heart that make the difference between success and failure. What you feel (or do not allow yourself to feel) is the energy that fuels or depresses your thoughts and actions. That energy is emotion. Emotion will hold your ideas in place and then colour your belief about a situation. It is the obstinacy that pushes up against the tide, the impatience that drives you crashing over the waterfall or the trust that floats you peacefully down river. Master your emotions and you will be the captain of your ship and the master of your fate.

Storytime

Some years ago I received a phone call from a friend who was worried about her six-year-old son Louis. He had watched a disaster movie during which an elevator had crashed to the bottom of the shaft, killing all the occupants. The following night he had a nightmare and was now terrified of getting into the elevator in his apartment block. As my friend lived on the tenth floor Louis's terror was not only upsetting for himself and his family but also inconvenient as someone had to carry him up the ten flights of stairs several times a day.

Later on that year Louis and his mother came to stay with me for a few days. Louis was a very bright, inquisitive child. He was always full of questions, especially those that related to his favourite movies and TV programmes. These happened to be *ET*, *Star Wars*, *Star Trek* and *Flight of the Navigator*. Louis's crying ambition and deepest wish was to fly in a spaceship. At bedtime, just before lights out, he would ask me to tell him stories about the stars and outer space. We would sit together on his bed and imagine we were cruising the universe in a space craft. Every night the fantasy became more and more detailed until after a week we almost believed it was real.

On the last day of Louis's holiday I took him to the mall. We had become good friends and I wanted to buy him a parting gift. He asked for a model of Battle Star Galactica so we headed for the toy department. And that was when the problem started. The escalators were being repaired; they were roped off and out of commission. We had to use the lift. Louis froze. I took his hand and walked forward toward the silver doors. Louis started to scream as his knees buckled and he sank to the floor. I was shocked and surprised. In a flurry of embarrassment I picked him up and raced for the mother-and-baby room. Safely behind a locked door I wiped away his tears and asked him: 'What happened?' 'The lift might crash,' he sniffed. 'We'll die.' 'Ahhh,' I said, and then out of nowhere I asked: 'What do you think it feels like to take off in a space ship?' 'I don't know,' he said pouting. 'Would you like to find out?' Louis lit up. 'How?' he said, his eyes as big as saucers. 'Well,' I said, whispering into his ear, 'this is a secret, but when you close your eyes and imagine you can fly into space, it feels just like going up in a high-speed lift.'

Louis and I headed for the soda fountain. Through the slurping of a triple chocolate milkshake we talked about warp-drives and transporters, gravity and tractor beams, take-off and re-entry, looping the loop around the sun. With the last drop of chocolate sucked through his straw Louis and I bravely walked across the concourse and stood in front of the elevator. I picked him up and said: 'Now remember to keep your eyes closed and think of a space ship.' There was a ding and a swish, swish as the doors opened and closed behind us. 'Ready for lift-off?' I whispered.

We spent the rest of the afternoon trying out every lift we could find. Louis went home without his present but with a gift that he would remember for the rest of his life.

It is time to continue training. The following paragraphs will exercise the bodymind. They have been designed to create a dialogue between the right and left side of your brain and between your conscious and unconscious mind. This reading exercise is written in such a way as to elicit images in your mind that will strengthen your self-awareness. To achieve the best results you will need to give yourself some private time and switch off the phone. Get comfortable and read slowly, taking time to pause at the end of each sentence. You may become aware of images, allow them to flow through your mind, and as you do so keep your body as still as you can. You should not act out any of the instructions, simply notice that they are there and what effect they may have. To begin with you may not notice anything significant. Remember you are on a training programme. This is one of many steps that will lead you towards your destination. You are putting a jigsaw together. Whether you know it yet or not, you have all the pieces, but you may not necessarily see the whole picture until all the parts are in place.

Sit comfortably on a chair in front of a desk or table. Your back should be supported and as straight as possible.

Take a deep breath and begin . . . As you look down at this page and refocus on these words it is easy to remember that you have read these words before. When you read you cannot help but focus your eyes on the words you are reading, and as you read you may be aware of the weight of this book as it rests in your hands. And how does this book feel to your hands as you hold it and read this text? Where do you notice the most pressure? Is it on the palm of one hand or on the other or do your fingertips take the weight of these type-filled pages? As you begin to discover exactly how you hold this book you may notice that you are making some adjustments with your hands and fingers. And can this book sit more comfortably in your hands? How much more comfortably can you hold this book as you read it?

You have two hands. Pay attention to them now. What positions do your fingers and thumbs take as they hold this book? Notice how they lie. How much more aware are you of one hand than the other as you read? Hands are very flexible. They have many different bones and many different joints. How many different ways can you use your hands in a day? Are the fingers equally flexible or are some fingers more flexible than others? Perhaps fingers can be like thoughts, some more flexible than others? How would it be for all your fingers to be as flexible as each other? What would it be like to be as flexible as you needed to be?

And have you noticed your hands? Do you know how your fingers adjust to the feel of the paper under your thumbs. Do your thumbs sense the same texture of paper as your other fingers as your eyes sweep across the page? Do you notice the weight of the book in your hands as you read? What would it be like to read a passage in a book and find that by reading your body can begin to relax. And what is it like to become aware that even as you breathe you can relax without even noticing? And I wonder how you will first begin to notice that you can feel relaxed as you read? And as you read how you will discover the answer to the questions that you have just read?

And you know reading is an interesting skill. You can discover so many things as you read. And as you look at the page you know that whenever you read your eyes will be focused on one word at a time, and yet at the very same moment they can also be reading several words ahead. Eyes are amazing things: they will see what is right in front of you and at the same time, they can record the quality of light and the other objects that surround you. As your eyes skim across this page what can you re-member about breathing and your mind and breathing and your body? And as you breathe what can you recall about breathing as you hold this book in your hands? Can you now notice the pace of your breathing or will it take a few more moments? And what can you notice about your breath as you pay attention to it now?

You have two feet. Notice how they rest upon the floor. How flat do these feet lie? How much more aware are you of one foot than the other? Like your hands, your feet are very flexible. They too have many different bones and many different joints. You know how to stand in many different ways. You can stand on tiptoes, resting all your weight on the spongy ball of your foot and your toes. You know, too, how to stand full square on the ground. Are the right toes as flexible as the right fingers? How do they move? You can raise a big toe on its own and they can be raised all together. How many other movements can these toes make without putting a strain on those feet? Have you noticed how you can sense different sensations in those toes and as you pay attention to the details in that part of this body you will find that you begin to notice that there can be many different levels of awareness at one time? You can be aware of the soles of those feet and recognize their sensitivity and at the same time realize that there are many small bones in those toes. You can be focused on those feet now and remember what they feel like as they walk barefoot on the grass.

You can be focused upon those feet and hear sounds. Some of these sounds will come from outside this body and some will be soundless like the words these eyes are reading on the page. Isn't it interesting how a soundless voice can have a tone and a rhythm. And now these ears know that they can hear a thought that has no sound and yet is not silent. And as you read you can feel the book in your hands and you can remember the feeling of holding this book before. As your eyes see the words on this page you know that you are rediscovering many things in many different ways. What is it like to discover that there are many different ways in which you can listen? You can listen to a memory and recall words of encouragement? What is it like to remember pleasant voices from the past? It is very easy to listen with your eyes as they read this page, and it can be easy to see how a pleasant word will alter sensations within your body. What would it be like to be able to listen to your body? How can you acquire greater awareness of your body so that you can listen to it? As you become curious about the messages that lie within it how will you continue to discover the many voices of your body?

You do remember the stories of your childhood. What favourite fairytales come to mind now as these eyes read this page evoking images from another time? How do they rest in the movie screen of your mind? These words can be seen with these eyes as they see the stories in mind stored within this memory. There are so many things occurring now. How do you hear and feel and see on many different levels at once? They can be experienced through sensations within your body. It is good to feel good, isn't it? There are so many routes to learning. A child can enjoy those stories and later on an adult can recognize and understand the very same story in a different way. In your own way reclaim all the pleasurable feelings and be secure in your ability to focus on confident and positive memories . . . And now you are discovering many different ways to learn and see and listen and discover.

So now you can remember how we started. Take a deep breath and look down at this page and refocus on these words. And as this passage comes to a close you will begin to refocus all your attention on the text right now. The words will somehow be clearer and sharper to your eyes as you listen to the words you read. And as you listen it is easy to remember that there is a strong link between mind and body. Your mind thinks and your body feels. When you pay good quality attention to yourself your mind and body thrive. Be more aware of your body now. How does the room sound? As you finish this sentence you can become absolutely wide awake. Alert and present now. Ready to stretch your body.

Take a deep breath and blow it out hard. Clap your hands now several times before you continue with your daily activities. As you stand take a few slow steps whilst being very aware of the sensation of the ground beneath your feet. Stand up and walk around the room to feel wide awake and focused on making the best of the rest of the day.

Some students noticed a positive change in their stance so pay attention to your posture as you walk and notice the pressure of your feet on the floor.

To master emotion lose control

7   *What if there was nothing wrong with me!*

OK, so what's wrong with you?

Tell me about it. Pick up your pad and write it all down. Do it now as you will need the information later. When you have finished read through your 'What Makes Me Feel Good?' list and get happy.

Imagine our world without the influence of Einstein and Plato, Alexander Graham Bell and Oppenheimer. Can you compare the theory of relativity, the philosophy of love, the birth of telecommunications and the harnessing of nuclear power and then conclude which has been more important in our evolution (or devolution for that matter)?

We all have a point of view. It is a matter of perspective and that is always coloured on the one hand by what we believe we need, and on the other by how we want to feel. Life and experience can be described in many different ways. Try this experiment. Right now from wherever you are look at the sky. (If you are reading in a subway this could be a problem. Close your eyes and remember the sky.) Observe that great roof above your head. What do your eyes see? You now know that you can feel your thoughts, so begin to recognize how you *feel* about what you see – how do you associate with the sky? What are you thinking about the sky now? What are your thoughts telling you about this experience?

Now write it down. Put pen to paper and record that sky in words and doodles. Try this experiment with a friend then compare notes. What did you discover?

Every picture tells a story and however you recount your story of the sky it will be very different from how it was recorded and remembered by your friend. Both were images of the sky, so who got it right, who saw the sky exactly as it was? *You were both right.* You both focused on recording what you saw and you saw what was important to you at that moment.

If you now look at the sky what do you see? Is it the same sky that you saw before? Sure it is, it just looks different now. Time has moved on. You can only see the first image of the sky in your mind. It is a memory. Look at the sky again, has it changed in the last few moments? Now you have another memory. Life is like that!

Now, try the experiment again with a group. Observe different things. TV commercials are great because they are short. You see them again and again and they are designed to have an impact. What about a football game? A painting in an art gallery? How different can your experience be? Your observations are distinct and valuable. The more you practise with this experiment the more you will discover your own and others' uniqueness. Is it fun to determine how another's insight can enhance your own? Where do you go for inspiration?

8 There is always a rainbow – it just takes a shower for us to notice

Look in the mirror. What can you see? That's you. Right here, right now, today this is how you are. On a scale of one to ten how do you feel about that? You may think: 'OK. Today I feel OK about myself.' Or you may be wishing you were someone else anywhere but here. Either way the message is:

What you see is what you get. Or is it – what you get is what you see?

What we are introducing here is the idea of ACCEPTANCE. This is the ability to recognize what's really going on in your life right now. It is the willingness to take off those rose-tinted glasses with their exaggerated frames, polish up the bedecked lenses and look at life through the lucidity of your uncovered eyes.

Let's face it – reality from time to time can seem harsh or cruel, uncomfortable or just downright boring. Sometimes and without thinking we can edit out something ugly or unpleasant, or add a little colour here and there to brighten things up.

Life can be challenging. It can be tough to come to terms with disappointment, particularly when your expectations of 'success' or 'happy ever after' don't turn out the way you envisioned. For some it is easier to live a life of 'If only . . . ', 'We'll be all right.', 'Just you wait till . . . ', 'Things aren't what they used to be,' or 'It can only get better' as they deny what's happening right under their noses, for good or bad, and fantasize fixedly on a fairytale future.

No matter how you may want things to be, right here and now this is how things are! Knowing this tiny fact is a vital component in your 'making a difference' kit. When you have the courage to see life for what it is right now and see a purpose in it, you will know what you need to change and how to go about doing it. Focused change is directed change and it will always get a positive result.

For every reason there's a purpose under heaven

What would happen if you suddenly discovered that 'life is a school'? What if, whether you like it or not, everything in your life is a lesson? What lessons are you learning? How do you feel about them? Are they useless or relevant, fun or challenging? What about those teachers? It's amazing the number of guises they can have. They come as parents, friends, lovers, children, bosses, partners, colleagues, competitors, therapists, antagonists and anyone else you can think of. They are disguised as weddings and funerals, illness and accidents, advancement and re-dundancy, success and failure, farewells and chance meetings, birth and regeneration. Wow, ain't life full of surprises!

So what about your life? What's going on that you are not too happy about? Pick on some minor irritation for now, you can tackle your greatest grievance later. Ponder on it for a while. Notice how you think and feel and then consider the following.

When confronted by life disguised as a lesson you have three main options. You can:

- Turn a blind eye – ignore the obvious
- Stay and struggle – complain or suffer
- Accept it – face up to the fact that there is a problem

What do you learn from ignoring the obvious?

- You're helpless
- You can't look after yourself
- You're not responsible

What do you learn from complaining or suffering?

- You don't have a choice
- You're a victim of circumstance

- Nothing changes
- No one cares

What can you learn from acceptance?
In this book acceptance does not mean agreement, corroboration, understanding, favouring, sympathizing, absolution, vindicating, justifying or aiding and abetting or giving in. Nor is it a passive state of compliance. It is:

- A standpoint before a change in action
- Letting go of an agenda
- Making room for unlimited possibility
- An opportunity to make the best and find the good in anything

When you accept things that you cannot change you free yourself up to focus on things that you can. When you know that you can make a difference you experience self-empowerment. When you are empowered you have the will, motivation and stamina to achieve your goals. With beliefs like that I guess you could succeed at anything you want!

Necessity is the mother of invention

For those of you who still need convincing, remember that you have completed many lessons to get this far. It took many faltering steps before you learned to walk with ease. Even then there were so many things to learn about standing on two feet. The lessons did not end. With some effort and a little time you learnt to hop and skip and jump and dance and run and leap. Perhaps you took your skill several steps higher and learned to climb a tree or scale a mountain or ski. You see the scope for growth is constant and endless. Just think if you had resisted learning to walk you would still be crawling around on all fours.

The more willing you are to embrace life's lessons the faster you will grow. If you dislike your problems and see the lessons as tiresome or stupid they will stay with you longer. Accept it. Resistance is useless.

When you are faced with an issue that is difficult to resolve ask yourself:

- What do I need to accept about this situation?
- What do I most need to learn about this?
- What perspective am I ignoring?
- What will be the benefit of change?
- What new skill can I develop to resolve this problem?
- How can I look after myself better?

9 *Basic revisited*

Right at the beginning of this book we talked about training, that is, taking steps, one at a time until you reach your desired result. Just like driving a car, to practise Emotional Excellence competently you will need to use several different skills simultaneously. Learning them individually is relatively simple. Synchronizing them takes a little time and plenty of practice. You have already come a long way and now is as good a time as any to check what you have learned so far. By participation in the following exercises you will have three opportunities:

- To review your progress
- To accept and appreciate your current skill level
- To learn a new skill

Before you get started you will need:

- Your lined pad
- A sketch pad
- Coloured pens and crayons
- Something to write with
- Uninterrupted time – set your answerphone please
- Somewhere comfortable to sit
- A rug – if you get cold when you relax
- Your basic training relaxation tape
- This book to hand

You are going to begin with your warm-up exercise. Remember this is the equivalent of stretching before a physical workout. It will help to release bodymind tension and oxygenate your brain. Read the exercise all the way through before you begin. Follow the instructions and then take it slowly.

Stand with your feet slightly apart – make sure they are parallel
Unlock (relax) your knees
Take a deep breath, fill your lungs
Blow out hard enough to make a good noise
Repeat this three times

Hold your position
As you breathe in deeply lift your right arm
Hold this pose for a slow count of four
Breathe out slowly and return your arm to a resting position
Repeat this breathing and stretch with the left arm
Now repeat the total movement three times for each side of your body

That was good. Well done.

Below is a bodychart. On courses we use them to record physical sensations and emotional responses that we have experienced during exercises. Here is an example of a bodychart filled in by a student who had just completed the exercise above.

You are going to use the bodychart below to record any areas of tension or tightness, discomfort and relaxation. Draw and colour in the sensations and feelings you have experienced. Remember to take as long as you need. When you have finished come back to the book.

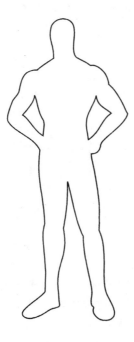

OK, great. How does your bodychart look?

Now go to your 'happy list'. Read the *first item* and then close your eyes and remember . . . enjoy the next few moments recalling that event in whatever way best suits you. Take about 30 seconds to experience this.

Now, using another bodychart, record in the form of words and doodles what you experienced. You can use as much or as little colour as you like. Take all the time you need to draw in the areas of relaxation, pleasure, changing sensations, discomfort, tension or tightness. Be as creative as you like.

OK, what did you notice as you were filling in your bodycharts? Were the charts the same or different in appearance? If they were different why do you think that is? Please keep a record of your results in your notebook as you may need to refer to it later.

Your pleasant memory will have evoked emotions and feelings that have in some way positively altered your physiology. How well can you change your life simply by monitoring your thoughts? What might happen for the best should you choose to spend more of your time thinking happy and positive thoughts?

> *It takes no more time*
> *to see the good side of life*
> *than it takes to see the bad.*
> Jimmy Buffett

10 What's the meaning of this?

Storytime

Once upon a time there was a little girl. She lived with her mother and father in a big house in a big city. Her daddy called her 'Princess' and carried her to bed every night on his shoulders and her mummy dressed her in white frilly dresses and shiny patent shoes.

When her parents were busy she would play in the nursery with her other young friends. After lunch they would all go to the park. Princess would be dressed in her favourite red dungarees and boots and walk to the playground with her very English nanny, her friends in tow. She enjoyed the park. She loved to stomp through piles of autumn leaves and to run face first into the wind. Princess prided herself on the fact that she could run faster and swing higher than any of the boys that dared her. She liked the swings and the roundabout but her favourite game was sliding head first down the big slide. This slide was so tall that when she reached the top, if she stood on tiptoes and out-stretched her arm as far as it would go, she could just touch the leaves of the old chestnut tree that grew in the graveyard which lay almost forgotten between the church of St Mary and the park.

One sunny day from her vantage point above the playground Princess stretched fearlessly toward her beloved chestnut tree. She was collecting conkers for her special friend Tom. Tom was very small and couldn't climb so high. Her fingertips brushed past breeze-blown leaves. She knew she could do it. It was easier this year because she was taller and stronger than the year before. She stretched and stretched especially high as the nannies sat peacefully watching their charges from the big round bench under the oak tree.

'Princess! Princess!' She heard a frightened shout from below. 'Princess. Just you come down right now or you'll fall.' The voice shook like the leaves that caressed her fingers. She looked towards the ground and saw her father's ashen face. Princess smiled. 'Look at me, I can touch the trees,' she laughed reassuringly. Her father's foot was on the ladder now. The giant slide shook under his urgent heavy steps. Princess grabbed the railings to steady herself. 'Be careful, Daddy,' she called protectively as the slide shuddered under his weight. 'Be careful,' he echoed from halfway up as the ladder buckled under his weight and he swung heavily to one side, pulling the ladder with him before he dropped to the ground. Princess tumbled through empty space like a stone from a sling. 'Daddy!' she called as she watched him fall.

It was a windblown winter's day. The cast was finally cut free from Princess's arm, revealing the weak, white spindly thing underneath. Princess, small hands snug in mittens, was wrapped up in her red-riding-hood coat and escorted to the park. 'Come, I'll push you on the swing,' the new nanny said, smiling. Princess had made some decisions. She shook her head. 'I can't.' She spoke quietly to the ground. 'Daddy won't like it.'

So what had happened to the fearless, curious child? She had, in a moment of intense emotion, replaced her natural curiosity with caution. Years later Princess explained herself. She had in her child's mind come to the crystal clear realization that in order to stay safe and to prevent her father from getting upset she must absolutely not take risks any more. Without realizing it, Princess had burdened herself with a ball and chain. By choosing to try to please others, Princess began to censor and edit out her own needs. She lost her authenticity and began to live with a fear of negative outcomes. The choice not to take risks soon became a habit and then a way of life. By the age of fifteen Princess was underachieving academically and socially and needed some help to regain her self-esteem. The outcome of that decision had had a negative impact on her life.

Whenever Princess came up against anything new an ever-watchful cautious voice would switch itself on. It had many ways of catching her attention. Sometimes it would replay a mind movie. This would look something like an image of her father's frightened face as he fell, mixed in with her own sense of fright and confusion. Perhaps a voice inside her head might say: 'What if you fall?' or 'Daddy will be angry if he sees you on that slide again.' Other times she might hear a disembodied voice saying harshly: 'It's all your fault.' 'Why were you so stupid?' 'Don't you dare do that again.' With thoughts and images like that running through your mind, it could be difficult to relax, take life as it comes and have fun, wouldn't you say?

If you don't use your mind it may abuse you!

So check out your thoughts. Make a decision now to find out which memories and the decisions associated with them work for you. Mentally put them in a file labelled 'Useful Experience'. As for the rest, box it, store it away and stamp it 'Outdated' and put it down to experience. After all, as Alexander Graham Bell found out when inventing the light bulb, 'if you don't make the odd mistake you don't make anything'!

If this sounds simple it is. Where did you get the idea that solutions and life, for that matter, had to be complicated? All you need to do is focus your attention on making a difference. To make a difference to your life right now make yourself comfortable. Set the answerphone to pick up your calls and put a 'do not disturb' sign on the door. Stretch your body and take some deep breaths until you feel that you have let go of some of your mental clutter. Now just sit down, either cross-legged or with both feet flat on the floor. Begin by reading the following passage slowly and rhythmically, pausing for breath at the end of each sentence. Remember you can gain some benefit from reading this passage, and you can gain a different benefit by committing it to tape and then listening to it with closed eyes.

Your eyes are now focused on the words you can read. As you listen to the words with inner ears you can remember other exercises that you have experienced in this book. And as you remember I wonder what you will recall? As you read you may already notice that your breathing has changed. What kind of rhythm can you breathe as you count to four? As you listen to the numbers with inner ears you may remember in your own way, how a natural breathing rhythm can relax your mind and body as you hold a book in your hands. Breathing rhythmically and slowly, you will recognize how the rise and fall of your chest can extend these growing sensations of relaxation. What kind of a relaxation is a relaxation like that? As you read this passage what level of relaxation have you reached now, and how much more deeply can your bodymind choose to relax as you continue to breathe rhythmically in and out? You may relax just a little bit more or you may observe even more comfort than you thought possible? How will it feel to be as relaxed and as comfortable as you can possibly be?

And as you relax your eyes are focused on the words you are reading. You can be aware of the feeling of this book as it rests in your hands. How does this book feel as you hold it in your hands? And how can you discover so many things by holding a book as you read? As you look at the page you know that whenever you read your eyes will be focused on one word at a time, and yet at the very same moment they can also be reading several words ahead. Eyes are amazing things, they will see what is right in front of you and at the same time, without really noticing, peripheral vision can record many other things in your environment. And as your eyes focus on this page what can you also notice about your surroundings? What else can you notice? You can notice the pace of your breathing whilst you sit and read? And what else can you notice? You can notice how your thoughts can be here and somewhere else at the same time. And what thoughts can enter your mind whilst you sit and read? How do your thoughts change as you read and discover new images in your mind? It is said that a picture can paint a thousand words. A picture that you see with inner eyes may be related to the words on the page. Perhaps you can see a picture evoked by a thought that has momentarily passed through your mind. I do not know what you can see in your mind, but I do know now that you know how to be in this room reading these words, and also be in your inner world of image and feeling and sound. And you can, by running your eyes over these words, simply exclude from your thoughts any information that you do not need to be aware of right now. Yet later if you need to re-member, you can recall all the information you need. And as you discover that you can lose a thought that you no longer need, you can also discover in your own special way how to hold on to thoughts that are happy and useful. And as you ponder, how can your mind discover in its own unique way what it would be like to lose a thought that had outlived its usefulness in your life? And what would it be like to find new and useful thoughts in your conscious mind? And what is it like to listen to a useful thought with inner ears? And you are reading so many questions? And I wonder how a question can help you to bring new and useful thoughts to mind. Your mind is a special place. I wonder what kind of thoughts your special mind could find useful. As your unconscious mind edits and erases the thoughts it no longer needs you can take all the time that you need to realize the benefit. As you benefit you already know that time can seem to stretch and shrink. Your awareness of time and space is altered with each task that you have accomplished, and with each accomplishment you can feel good about the fact that you spent just the right amount of time on it.

Now listen to your breath. And take a deep breath now. Your chest can rise and fall as you recognize that there has been a change in your level of relaxation. Your mind may begin to wander as you wonder what you have gained from reading this text. And as you breathe deeply, that wondering can help you to integrate any new learning into everyday awareness so that you can discover the many benefits in your own way.

You have been reading and you are reading now and listening to the words that your eyes can see. And your mind knows where it stores all your special memories. And because your mind knows these things, you can have a special memory that makes you feel so good. And as you feel so good you can become more and more aware of how it is that you can recall such special moments in your life. Each special memory has its own images and feelings and sensations. You are learning now how easy it is to learn something about yourself that you did not know. And as you get to know more about the places in your mind where you have good memories you can begin to recall a time when learning something was very easy. It is so very interesting to discover that learning can be an agreeable experience. What kind of agreeable learning experience might that be? How can that agreeable experience develop? It is so comfortable to know that a positive learning from the past can teach you so much in the present. And I wonder what kind of present you can have? And what kind of a present is a present like that? What could be the best way of using a present like that?

Your mind knows many wonderful things about you that you are just beginning to find out. And in what way can your wonderful mind continue to discover new things from a positive learning experience? And you have discovered that your mind is a vast place in which you can store many things. And as you explore these places you will discover more and more ways that you can do many things so easily. And now you know you have an inner explorer who really enjoys seeking out positive outcomes to all your queries and questions. And as you remember how to count from one to four you may recall that rhythmic breath. And the inner explorer knows that rhythm too. And it is so easy to remember how to seek positive outcomes as you relax and breathe. What kind of positive outcomes are positive outcomes like that? And as your inner mind decides you can find yourself wondering how you will continue to benefit as you come to full waking awareness now. Taking deep, deep breaths as you read the words on the page. And as you notice the rhythm of your breath you know that your heart beats to a rhythm too. And with the rhythm of each heartbeat blood flows easily through your veins taking oxygen to all parts of your body. And that oxygen is fuel that can flow deep into your body filling every cell, and as it flows, it is so very easy, to just let go of pockets self-doubt and tension which can leave your body with each outward breath. And you can wonder how much benefit you can receive from a rhythmic breath that flows through your body in this way as you breathe in and out. And you can receive all the

benefit that you need in a very short time of between two to five minutes. And as you finish this paragraph you can find yourself closing your eyes as you take some time to sit quietly and integrate new realizations as rhythm flows through your body. Your mind knows about time and can measure the benefit of five minutes of breathing before you open your eyes. And when it is time for your eyes to open it is so easy to remember how to seek positive outcomes. And you can really feel the benefit of taking the time as you come to full waking awareness once again.

Be aware of the room around you now and focus on your feet. You can feel the floor beneath you. Now focus on your feet and as you feel your feet flex and wiggle your toes. Stretch your body. Breathe in deeply and blow out hard. And again breathe deeply in and blow out hard. Be ready to *stretch your body and open your eyes*. Look around you. What colours can you see? That was an interesting exercise. Well done. Clap your hands hard together for a few moments. Great. Now for something completely different.

Make a list of all the times you have succeeded in learning something new. For example learning to talk (yes, I really do mean everything).

Then make a list of how that new skill has benefited your life. For example, talking helps you to make friends, give a speech, sing, act in a play, order a pizza – get the idea?

Here is an example list for you to follow:

- Learning to read means I can understand and function better in the outside world. It also gives me the opportunity to educate myself.
- Learning to cook means I can feed myself well and entertain family and friends with endless delicious dishes.

- Getting dumped by my partner has not only given me insight into my relationship patterns but allows me to see whoever I want and discover what I enjoy doing as a single person.
- Moving to a different area has broadened my horizons and introduced me to a new social circle.
- Breaking my leg gave me an opportunity to rest and reflect on how rushed and pressurized my life had become.
- Learning to type benefited me by broadening my employment prospects and allowed me to learn lots of new computer skills.
- Learning how to put on make-up helps me make the best of myself and makes me feel more attractive as a woman.
- Learning about how polluted the world is gave me the choice to live a healthier lifestyle and encouraged a sense of responsibility to the environment, myself and the community.
- The death of my sister forced me to reach out and accept support from others. I am now a more compassionate and loving person.
- Changing my job provided a more intellectually challenging working environment in which I am making new friends and gaining confidence.

Remember sometimes tough and uncomfortable lessons can teach you self-empowering skills too. Occasionally, being bullied can teach you to stand up for yourself. Some of the funniest people learnt the art of humour to hide their insecurity. Laughter is the best medicine. Gaining self-esteem can show you that the world is laughing with you and not at you.

Just because something feels bad doesn't mean you can't make some good out of it

11 *Influential thinking*

Once you were a very small child. A tiny, totally dependent human being whose ongoing survival and success was based on the fact that you had an incredible capacity to learn and to remember. You were an open vessel just waiting to be filled. And what were you filled with? Ideas and experience, of course! And where did these come from? Conceivably, the answer lies in the beliefs and behaviour of significant others such as parents, friends and family, teachers or religious figures; or from the social influences we have been subjected to, like TV shows, cartoons, advertising, the school playground, family get-togethers, computer games, books, magazines, comic books, movies, Walt Disney, the Internet and more. The list of available information sources is innumerable and mind-boggling. Can you imagine programming the world's most powerful and unique computer with random bits of unsolicited and disorganized information? We are that computer overflowing with hit-or-miss data. It is the stuff that your life is made of!

Every one of us has random passive thoughts babbling away in that space between our ears. In any lifetime we hear billions of soundless voices commenting on everything from the colour of toilet tissue to the latest global crisis. Thoughts can have different qualities; sometimes they are pleasant, exciting and evocative and at other times they can be rude, frightening or downright stubborn. You will have already encountered the influence of peaceful and happy thoughts. Furthermore, you know from experience how unhappy, frustrated, stressed-out thinking affects you too. Whatever internal chatter you find yourself listening to, one thing is certain, it will have a significant impact on your state of mind, your health and your emotions.

You are the ultimate influence in your life.
Inspire yourself wisely.

So what influences you? How do you know? Have you ever reviewed the contents of your mind? When did you last check if you were running the most efficient programme to achieve your goals? Remember, thought is powerful. It influences your emotions, and emotion is the rudder that steers you across the ocean of life.

✍ (You will find this rather enlightening)
Go to a café, bar or some other place where people congregate. Take a note pad and pen, find somewhere where you can sit for a while, order a drink or whatever you like and just observe and listen. I know that it is considered rude to eavesdrop, but hey, this is a public place, so the conversation won't be too private. What do people say? How do they talk about themselves, others, life, work, college? Make a few notes. What kind of statements do they make? What kind of questions do they ask? Do you hear anything familiar?

So what did you hear? 'Have you heard the news? And isn't life hard? And what's the world coming to?'

OK, so this may be an extreme example, but you get the point, right?

And guess what! Your external chatter mirrors your internal chatter and vice versa. We make statements that criticize, compare, analyse, justify, vilify, gossip, belittle and judge – not only others, but ourselves too.

And after all this talk we will often conclude that our perspective is right, and we continue to be right until we are told we are wrong; and then we become even more right, or we doubt ourselves horribly. And where does that get us?

Could it be that people talk about others in a vain attempt to avoid sorting out their own lives? Complaining can be a very effective way of side-stepping responsibility and a perfect cover for avoiding change. Furthermore, moaning takes up a whole lot of time and energy that you could be using to make a difference! So how can you become aware of these self-sabotage strategies and free up this available energy to utilize it productively? I am certain that you will come up with some great ideas of your own. In the meantime while you are waiting for them to appear try these.

Idea 1
Be aware of how you express yourself. Keep an ear open for the things you and others say repetitively. During your conversations with people listen to the way you talk when you are dissatisfied in some way. Notice how you talk to your children, friends, family, colleagues, students; what are they learning about you from the words you speak? What kind of impact are you having?

Idea 2
Take responsibility for how you think. Whenever you find yourself being critical or derisory about anything ask yourself 'Is there anything that I am avoiding right now?' If you get an affirmative answer focus your attention in that direction with the intention to have a positive impact on the situation of concern. What kind of beneficial result could you see?

Idea 3
Be discerning about what you listen to. In the outside world you do this all the time. When you don't like what you hear on the radio do you keep listening or adjust the dial to another frequency? What about TV, do you watch the same station all the time? Of course not. You skip through the options and decide on whatever takes your fancy.

And now another reading exercise which will help you to discover how you can quieten an active mind. You can gain some benefit from reading this slowly and you can gain a different benefit by committing the following passage to tape then listening to it with closed eyes. Now, make yourself comfortable, either cross-legged or with both feet flat on the floor. Begin by reading slowly and rhythmically. Remember to pause for breath at the end of each sentence.

You have been reading and you are reading now and listening to the words that your eyes can see. Even as you read the words you may become aware of an inner commentary whilst at the same time being aware of sounds that surround you. As you listen to the words with inner ears you can remember other exercises that you have experienced in this book. And what do you recall about breathing? And what kind of breathing can you do to the count of four? And as you listen with inner ears and remember breathing to the count of four you may re-member in your own way how a natural breathing rhythm can relax your mind and body. And as you recall what it is like to breathe rhythmically and slowly you will recognize how the rise and fall of your chest can extend these growing sensations of relaxation. How does your relax-ation evolve? And what kind of a relaxation is a relaxation like that? What level of relaxation have you reached now and how much more deeply will your bodymind choose to relax as you continue to breathe rhythmically in and out? Will it be just a little more or will you relax even further than you have managed to relax before? How will it feel to be as relaxed and as comfortable as you can be? And what kind of breathing can you do to the count of four? And as you listen to the rhythm with inner ears, and remember breathing to that count, you may also have a memory of choosing a happy thought. And what kind of a happy thought was a happy thought like that which your mind and body can experience in their own special way? And as you experience those special sensations you can encounter that memory with inner eyes. And what kind of a special encounter is an encounter like that as your inner vision becomes clearer and clearer (pause here as your inner vision develops).

And now you know you can find an image for your inner eyes to see that becomes clearer and clearer like a blue blue sky on a warm summer day . . . and you can wonder where seeing inner eyes can find a fluffy white white cloud in a blue blue sky on a warm summer day. And you can have a sense of curiosity about a fluffy white cloud as your inner eyes see light. And as you breathe, you can wonder how would it feel to breathe light into your body from a fluffy white cloud as it gets closer and closer now . . . And what kind of feeling is a feeling of breathing in light? What pleasant sensations can you notice as you absorb that light into your body? And as you notice the rhythm of your breath you know that your heart beats to a rhythm too. And with the rhythm of each heartbeat that light can flow deep into your body, filling every cell, and as that light flows, it is so very easy to just let go of pockets of tension or tightness which leave your body with each outward breath. And you can wonder how much benefit you can receive from a rhythmic light that flows through your body in this way as you breathe in and out. And you can receive all the benefit that you need in a very short time of between two to five minutes. Your mind knows about time and can measure the benefit of five minutes of breathing a bright light and then remind you to open your eyes.

And just as you look at words you can read. Your inner eyes can be focused on an inner light that fills every part of your body. As you listen to the words with inner ears you can remember other exercises that you have experienced in this book. And as you remember I wonder what you will recall about releasing pockets of tension or tight-ness which leave your body with each outward breath? And as you remember you may already notice that your breathing has changed. And what kind of rhythm can you breathe as you receive a rhythmic light that flows through your body as you breathe in and out? And as you see a breathing light you may remember in your own way how a natural breathing rhythm can relax your mind and body as you hold a book in your hands. And as you recall what it is like to breathe rhythmically and slowly, you will recognize how the rise and fall of your chest can extend these growing sensations of relaxation. And what kind of a relaxation is a relaxation like that? And how much more deeply can your bodymind choose to relax as you continue to breathe rhythmically in and out? You may relax just a little bit more or you may observe even more comfort than you thought possible. How will it feel to be as relaxed and as comfortable as you can possibly be? And as you relax you can wonder how much benefit you can receive from a rhythmic light that flows through your body in this way. And you can receive all the benefit that you need in a very short time of between two to five minutes. Your mind knows about time and can measure the benefit of five minutes of breathing a bright light and then remind you to open your eyes. And as you finish this paragraph you can find yourself closing your eyes as you take some time to sit quietly and receive a rhythmic light that flows through your body. And when it is time for your eyes to open you can really feel the relief of taking the time to rest, and release from your bodymind all that you no longer need as you come to full waking awareness once again.

Focus on your feet. You can feel the floor beneath you. Now focus on your feet and as you feel them flex and wiggle your toes. Stretch your body. Breathe in deeply and blow out hard. And again breathe deeply in and blow out hard. Be ready to *stretch your body and open your eyes.* Look around you. What colours can you see? That was an illuminating experience. Well done. Now do something physical like washing the dishes or walking the dog.

We often say 'let's shed a little light on the situation' when we are troubled or confused. When someone is depressed, angry or intense we tell them to 'lighten up'. Now you have acquired the art of light breathing you can re-create light at any time. You can better your experience of any event whether real or imagined whenever you feel the need.

There is never a darkness so deep that a candle cannot illuminate it

12   *It's all talk*

Now I know that particular noises can seem much louder than others. These are usually related to strong emotions such as anxiety, guilt, worry, anger, resentment, confusion, anticipation, passion, and believe it or not, love in all its guises. These are feelings of attachment, they are evocative, often compelling and they can exert a powerful influence on what you think, feel and do. On the other hand, the sound can be pervasive like canned music, seemingly innocuous, wafting in and out of our awareness from the background of our mind. You may be so familiar with the sound that you take its influence for granted and barely notice its effect, until you want to play another tune that is.

I like to think of this plethora of sound and emotion as nothing more than a tribe of chattering monkeys. I know that monkeys can be noisy, irritating, mischievous, contrary and argumentative from time to time. They can and usually do sound something like the chatter on the next page.

I also understand that this particular bunch bounce around in your brain and take turns to sit on your shoulder and shout in your ear. However, if you are willing to take the time to tame and civilize them a little you will discover a playful, intelligent, loving and comical side to their nature that can be a bonus and a benefit.

Let us begin to work with the idea you read about in Chapter 8 'There is always a rainbow – it just takes a shower for us to notice.'

However authoritative or formidable those words seem to be and whatever you understand them to mean at this moment, I believe that at the time of delivery they were intended to be helpful.

"YOU'RE TOO YOUNG TO UNDERSTAND."   "You must be on time."

"Why can't you be like your brother."   "Don't do that, dear, it's not nice."

"It's all your fault!"

"Men don't make passes at girls who wear glasses."

"We've sacrificed so much for you."   "You're not trying hard enough."

"Don't let me down again."   "We're very disappointed in you."

"I expected more from you than that."   "That's not a proper job."

"Don't be so stupid."   "You've failed us!"

"You should be pleased."   "You are such an embarrassment."

"You can't do that!"   "YOU'LL CATCH YOUR DEATH OF COLD."

"Don't think you're going out dressed like that, young lady!"

"You're too young to be in love."   "You should be thinner, prettier, cleverer, faster...."

"You don't know what you're talking about!"

"This will be more painful for me than it will be for you."

"Whose going to marry you?"   "Stop crying, you're getting hysterical."

"You're all talk and no action."   "Don't bother me now."   "Will you behave!"

"Be grateful for what you've got."   "Don't talk back to me!"

"DON'T CARE WAS MADE TO CARE."   "Run along now"

"You never learn."   "Just wait til your father gets home!"

"Don't cry, you'll be alright."   "I want doesn't get."   "And don't be late."

"He's not good enough for you."   "You need to lose a few pounds."

"You will do as you're told."   "Speak when you're spoken to.

"Who do you think you are?"   "GROW UP!"

"Big boys don't cry."   "Don't be so childish."   "Be quiet!"

"Don't be so silly."   "You're so unhelpful."   "You must learn to respect your elders."

"What if something should happen to you?"   "What will I do without you?"

"Don't make me have to smack you."   "Be a good boy."

"Be careful!"   "Pull yourself together!"

I also understand that although those words may have been severe, judgemental, apprehensive, obstructive or opposing they were not necessarily meant to be thoughtless or unkind. On the contrary, they are often spoken by people who care for us deeply. People who wish to protect us from getting hurt. People who want to see the best for us and believe that they have our best interest at heart.

It is something of a paradox. The very words that were meant in fact to protect us (from our own folly, of course) may have such a controlling, undermining and contrary effect on our lives that we never acknowledge or strive for our true potential.

When dealing with my own tribe of chattering monkeys I find it useful to remember that our parents and elders, although our equals, are not always our betters. They were and are also re-cipients of thoughtless, controlling behaviour. As were their parents and teachers. We are all from time to time the casualties and perpetrators of emotional damage. We all experience fear and we often disguise it as a concern for someone else's well-being. We are all potential victims of other people's ideas or perceptions of:

- What is right or wrong
- Who you are
- How they want you to be
- Who they want you to become
- What they expect you to achieve
- What they believe you can or cannot accomplish
- What they believe you should or should not do
- What they believe you should know
- What they believe you should think
- Their responsibility as a parent, teacher, friend, mentor

It is important to realize that we have all colluded with each other in this particular 'game of life'. We have all experienced the powerful influence of the 'voice of disapproval'. We fear the thought and the consequence of embarrassment, condemnation, failure and letting someone down. The closer we are to breaking the rules, changing the game and making a difference, the greater the pressure of noise from those chattering monkeys.

If you let them, they can and will drown out your own inner voice that lets you know what is right for you. And if taken to heart those fears will act like a cholesterol cork which will obstruct your arteries and restrict the flow of spontaneity, love, creativity and abundance.

Surely you carry enough doubts of your own,
do you really need to put others in your rucksack?

So how do we break the patterns from the past? How do we take control of those voices and regain emotional (and therefore physical) health and vitality?

The answer is to change your diet. Exercise your right to think for yourself. Go for a lifestyle change. Quieten your mind using the relaxation and breathing exercises you taped in Chapters 1 and 4.

And now another reading exercise which will help you to dissipate some of that internal chatter, and steady your emotions. You can gain some benefit from reading this slowly and you can gain a different benefit by committing the following passage to tape then listening to it with closed eyes. Now, make yourself comfortable, either cross-legged or with both feet flat on the floor. Begin by reading slowly and rhythmically. Remember to pause for breath at the end of each sentence.

As you turn the page and refocus on these words it is easy to discover more about yourself as you read. You cannot help but focus your attention on the words you are reading, and you may be aware of the feeling of this book as it rests in your hands. And how does it feel to hold this book as you read the text? Where do you notice the most pressure? Is it on the palm of one hand or the other, or do your fingertips take the weight of these type-filled pages? And as you begin to discover exactly how you hold this

book you may notice that you are making some adjustments with your hands and fingers. And how much more comfortably can you hold this book as you read it? And you are reading so many questions. I wonder how curious you can be about the words you will see as your eyes skim across this page. And what will you read next as you notice how your arms adjust to the weight of the book in your hands? What would it be like to read a passage in a book and to find that just by reading your body could begin to relax? And what is it like to discover that even as you read the muscles in your face can relax? And I wonder how you will discover the answer to the questions that you have just read? And you know reading is an interesting skill. You can discover so many things as you read. And as you look at the page you know that whenever you read your eyes will be focused on one word at a time, and yet at the very same moment they can also be reading several words ahead. Eyes are amazing things, they will see what is right in front of you and at the same time, whether you realize it or not, your peripheral vision can record the quality of light and the other objects in your environment. And as your eyes focus on this page what can you also notice about your surroundings? What can you notice? You can notice how your thoughts can be here and somewhere else at the same time. And what thoughts enter your mind whilst you sit and read? How do your thoughts change as you read and discover new images in your mind? Every thought you have can create some image. It may be related to the words on the page or it could be an image evoked by a thought that has momentarily passed through your mind. I do not know what you can see in your mind, but I do know that you can recognize now that you can be in this room reading this material, and at the same time be in your own world of image and sound. Thus simply by running your eyes over the typeface in front of you, you can exclude information that you do not need to be aware of right now. Yet later if you need to remember what was going on in the room you will be able to see the room again in your mind's eye as a memory, and recall all the information you need. You already know that time can seem to stretch and shrink. Have you noticed how long a kettle takes to boil when you watch it and how fast time seems to move when you are having fun? Your awareness of time and space is altered with each task that you have accomplished, and with each accomplishment you can feel good about the fact that you spent just the right amount of time on it. Now listen to your breath – take a deep breath now. Your chest can rise and fall as you recognize that there has been a change in your level of relaxation. Your mind may begin to wander as you wonder what new methods of learning you may have gained from reading this text. And as you breathe deeply that wondering can help you to integrate any new learning into everyday awareness so that you can discover the many benefits in your own way. You can begin to refocus all your attention on the text right now as you once again find yourself present here, aware of your body and any sounds around you.

You have been reading and you are reading now and listening to the words that your eyes can see. Even as you read the words you may become aware of an inner commentary whilst at the same time being aware of sounds that surround you. As you listen to the words with inner ears you can remember other exercises that you have experienced in this book. And what do you recall about breathing? And what kind of breathing can you do to the count of four? And as you listen with inner ears and remember breathing to the count of four you may remember in your own way how a natural breathing rhythm can relax your mind and body. And as you recall what it is like to breathe rhythmically and slowly you will recognize how the rise and fall of your chest can extend these growing sensations of relaxation. How does your relaxation evolve? And what kind of a relaxation is a relaxation like that? What level of relaxation have you reached now and how much more deeply will your bodymind choose to relax as you continue to breathe rhythmically in and out? Will it be just a little more or will you relax even further than you have managed to relax before? How will it feel to be as relaxed and as comfortable as you can be? And what kind of breathing can you do to the count of four? And as you listen to the rhythm with inner ears, and remember breathing to that count, you may also have a memory of choosing a happy thought. And what kind of a happy thought was a happy thought like that which your mind and body can experience their own special way. And as you experience those special sensations you can encounter that memory with inner eyes. And what kind of a special encounter is an encounter like that as your inner vision becomes clearer and clearer (pause here as your inner vision develops).

And now you know you can find an image for your inner eyes to see that becomes clearer and clearer like a blue blue sky on a warm summer day . . . and you can wonder where seeing inner eyes can find a fluffy white white cloud in a blue blue sky on a warm summer day. And you can have a sense of curiosity about a fluffy white cloud as your inner eyes see light. And as you breathe, you can wonder how would it feel to breathe light into your body from a fluffy white cloud as it gets closer and closer now . . . And what kind of feeling is a feeling of breathing in light? What pleasant sensations can you notice as you absorb that light into your body? And as you notice the rhythm of your breath you know that your heart beats to a rhythm too. And with the rhythm of each heartbeat that light can flow deep into your body filling every cell, and as that light flows, it is so very easy, to just let go of pockets of tension or tightness which leave your body with each outward breath. And you can wonder how much benefit you can receive from a rhythmic light that flows through your body in this way as you breathe in and out. And you know what it is like to breathe rhythmically and slowly. And you can discover how the rise and fall of your chest can draw a rhythmic light into your body. And how does a sensation of expanding light lead to relaxation? And what kind of a relaxation is a relaxation like that? What level of relaxation have you reached now and how much more deeply will your bodymind choose to relax as you continue to breathe light rhythmically in and out? Will it be just a little more or will you relax even further than you have managed to relax before? How will it feel to be as relaxed and as comfortable as you can be? And what kind of comfortable breathing can you do to the count of four? And what kind of a peaceful voice is a peaceful voice like that? And I do not know what your inner peaceful voice might say. But I do know that you can wonder at the wisdom of a peaceful voice that lies within the landscape of your mind. It is a quiet, gentle voice. And when your ears are open you can listen to a quiet, gentle voice inside your mind. You may hear it as the rustle of a breeze or from a bubbling brook or in a bird song. It may be as silent as a bluebell growing in the grass or the fragrance of a rose bathed in sunlight. And you can wonder if there is a message in the soft pitter patter of a raindrop or the tap, tap, tapping of the woodpeckers in the woods. And as you listen to the rhythm with inner ears, and remember breathing to a count, you can wonder about a peaceful voice that lives in your mind. And I wonder what is an inner voice like that? And how does a peaceful magical voice that lives within the landscape of your mind converse with your bodymind? And how does your bodymind listen to that voice in its own special way? And you can discover this voice is full of wisdom. And as you discover you may find that a voice like that can answer any question you may ask. And as you listen to your breath you can remember that a quiet, gentle voice inside your mind will only talk when you are willing to listen. And how does a peaceful voice talk to your bodymind? And how does your bodymind listen to a peaceful voice that it can hear in its own special way? And now you know that in a peaceful inner voice can be an image for your inner eyes to see and a sound for your inner ears to hear.

And as you finish this paragraph you can find yourself closing your eyes as you take some time to sit quietly and receive a rhythmic light that flows through your body as you breathe. And you can receive all the benefit that you need from a rhythmic light in a very short time. And your mind knows about time and can measure the benefit of five minutes of breathing a bright light. And as you finish this paragraph you can take five minutes to close your eyes and breathe. And your mind knows about time and can measure five minutes and with a quiet inner voice remind you to open your eyes. And when it is time for your eyes to open you can really feel the relief of taking the time to rest and release from your bodymind all that you no longer needed as you come to full waking awareness once again.

Focus on your feet. You can feel the floor beneath you. Now focus on your feet and as you feel them flex and wiggle your toes. Stretch your body. Breathe in deeply and blow out hard. And again breathe deeply in and blow out hard. Be ready to *stretch your body and open your eyes*. Look around you. What colours can you see? Clap your hands several times. That was an illuminating experience. Well done. Now do something physical like washing the dishes or walking the dog.

13 Mastering the monkeys

I have mentioned in previous chapters that life can be seen as a school. The difference between the school you went to in your younger years and 'life school' is that in school the subjects were set. There was a curriculum you were expected to follow, you were given homework and expected to sit and pass tests. In 'life school' the lessons may be more vague, there are no specific tests and you must learn to judge for yourself how you are doing. You learn by putting yourself in situations that challenge you. There is no right way to evolve or to discover your life's purpose. You can and will learn as much from apparent failures and disappointments as your apparent successes and achievements. You will never stop learning. Each lesson develops into the next just as spring follows winter.

In spite of society's current preoccupation with youth and vitality, we are all, like it or not, subject to the cycles of nature. If a seed could not listen to the message of spring it would not blossom. If an oak held fast to its leaves at the onset of winter it would break under the weight of its snow-laden branches.

There are messages all around us. Mastery is being able to determine which messages to pay attention to and which to ignore. You will be able to discriminate when you are willing to listen to your chattering monkeys with an open mind. Remember we can learn a lot from them. Their messages can remind us of the beliefs and memories that we hold on to. Negative attachments to the past can stunt our growth and prevent us from moving forward into successful futures. Difficult circumstances do not have to be disastrous. You have the ability to learn something positive from a painful event. Something that you may not have learnt without it.

How can you discover courage if you do not experience fear? How would you learn to trust if you never took a risk? How would you appreciate the value of success if you had never experienced failure? How will you know your own truth if you are not willing to question the truth of others?

Having said all that, I recognize that these monkeys can be pests. They will, if you don't know how to stop them, interrupt your intentions for change and fill your mind with all sorts of undermining scenarios. Listening to them is a habit and the best way to break a habit is to create another one to take its place.

Here are some exercises on mind mastery that I give to students on my courses. It will lessen the impact that your monkeys have on your life.

- Change the way you perceive and experience them. Use your imagination, give those voices a face, put clown make-up on them and give them lollipops to keep their mouths busy.
- Play with the sound. Speed up the noise until all you hear is a high-pitched babble. Slow it down so the words deepen and drag. Try running them backwards and forwards at high speed.
- If you are unsure about the messages you are receiving, ask yourself:
  'Does this thought/idea/image support me in achieving my goals?'
  'Is this thought/idea/image an opportunity to grow?'
  'Will this thought/idea/image enhance my life?'
- Take control. Decide what you want to hear. Silence those monkey voices with some powerful self-talk, like so:
  for every negative or unproductive thought you have about yourself or your abilities counteract it with something positive, motivating or loving. Now record your new messages over the old ones.

  You have the ability to know your own truth; follow your own guidance

One of the great benefits of mind mastery is that you will begin to recognize the great variety of thoughts that pass through it. Furthermore, you will quickly notice the effect that they have on your body. You will become more aware of your posture, your movements, your emotions and how all of these affect your behaviour and the way you communicate.

You already have a direct experience of a train of inner thought, loaded with chattering monkeys that ride on a clattering roller coaster of tension, anticipation, fear, acceleration and apprehension that:

- Make you wrong
- Tell you that your efforts are not enough
- Impose impossible deadlines that make you rush
- Tell you that you've failed
- Find fault rather than seeing the good

For short bursts of time the ride can be exciting and exhilarating, but can you imagine never being able to get off?

You will have discovered that by practising the exercises above you can alter and interrupt your inner dialogue. It can take many years of ongoing observation and intent to bring your mind to a constant state of stillness and focus. However, as you practise these skills you will learn to master your mind. The result is that your mind learns to obey rather than control you. We all have to start from somewhere and here is as good a place as any.

As you turn the page and refocus on these words it is easy to discover more about yourself as you read. You cannot help but focus your attention on the words you are reading, and you may be aware of the feeling of this book as it rests in your hands. And how does it feel to hold this book as you read the text? Where do you notice the most pressure? Is it on the palm of one hand or the other or do your fingertips take the weight of these type-filled pages? And as you begin to discover exactly how you hold this

book you may notice that you are making some adjustments with your hands and fingers. And how much more
comfortably can you hold this book as you read it? And
you are reading so many questions. I wonder how curious
you can be about the words you will see as your eyes skim
across this page. And what will you read next as you
notice how your arms adjust to the weight of the book in
your hands? What would it be like to read a passage in a
book and to find that just by reading your body could
begin to relax? And what is it like to discover that even as
you read the muscles in your face can relax? And I wonder
how you will discover the answer to the questions that you
have just read? And you know reading is an interesting
skill. You can discover so many things as you read. And as
you look at the page you know that whenever you read
your eyes will be focused on one word at a time, and yet at
the very same moment they can also be reading several
words ahead. Eyes are amazing things, they will see what
is right in front of you and at the same time, whether you
realize it or not your peripheral vision can record the
quality of light and the other objects in your environment.
And as your eyes focus on this page what can you also
notice about your surroundings? What can you notice?
You can notice the pace of your breathing whilst you sit
and read. What can you notice? You can notice how your
thoughts can be here and somewhere else at the same
time. And what thoughts enter your mind whilst you sit
and read? How do your thoughts change as you read and
discover new images in your mind? Every thought you
have can create some image. It may be related to the words
on the page or it could be an image evoked by a thought
that has momentarily passed through your mind. I do not
know what you can see in your mind, but I do know that
you can recognize now that you can be in this room
reading this material, and at the same time be in your own
world of image and sound. Thus simply by running your

eyes over the typeface in front of you, you can exclude information that you do not need to be aware of right now. Yet later if you need to remember what was going on in the room you will be able to see the room again in your mind's eyes as a memory, and recall all the information you need. You already know that time can seem to stretch and shrink. Have you noticed how long a kettle takes to boil when you watch it and how fast time seems to move when you are having fun? Your awareness of time and space is altered with each task that you have accomplished, and with each accomplishment you can feel good about the fact that you spent just the right amount of time on it. Now listen to your breath – take a deep breath now. Your chest can rise and fall as you recognize that there has been a change in your level of relaxation. Your mind may begin to wander as you wonder what new methods of learning you may have gained from reading this text. And as you breathe deeply that wondering can help you to integrate any new learning into everyday awareness so that you can discover the many benefits in your own way.

And as you discover you are reading and listening to the words that your eyes can see. Even as you read the words you can become aware of an inner commentary. And you have listened with inner ears before. And as you listen you can remember now other exercises that you have experienced in this book. And as you listen with inner ears and remember breathing to the count of four you may remember in your own way how a natural breathing rhythm can relax your mind and body. And as you recall what it is like to breathe rhythmically and slowly you will recognize how the rise and fall of your chest can extend these growing sensations of relaxation. How does your relaxation evolve? And now how much more deeply will your bodymind choose to relax as you continue to breathe rhythmically in and out? How will it feel to be as relaxed and as comfortable as you can be? And as you listen to the rhythm of your breath, with inner ears, and remember breathing to that count, you may also have a memory of choosing a happy thought. And what kind of a happy thought was a happy thought like that which your mind and body can experience their own special way? And as you experience those special sensations you can now breathe deeply and have a happy experience that can help you to synthesize new learning into everyday awareness. And now you can discover the many benefits in your own way. And in your own way you can begin to refocus all your attention on the text right now as you once again find yourself present here, aware of your body and any sounds around you. And breathe in deep and focus on your feet. And as you focus your attention will be here more and more.

Now breathe and focus on your feet. You can feel the floor beneath you. Now focus on your feet and as you feel them flex and wiggle your toes. Stretch your body. Breathe in deeply and blow out hard as if you were blowing out candles on a birthday cake. Good. Breathe in again and blow out even harder this time. Great. *Now stretch your body and open your eyes*. Look around you. What colours can you see? Clap your hands hard together several times before you continue with your day. Well done. Now do something physical like washing the dishes, mowing the lawn, walking the dog or working out.

14   *Silence is golden*

Within the landscape of your mind, not far from the place where the chattering monkeys live is another voice. It is a quiet, gentle voice. When your ears are open you can hear it in the breeze as it rustles past the trees. It may be talking from a bubbling brook or through a bird song. Have you ever wondered if there was a message in the pitter patter of raindrops or the tap, tap, tap of the woodpecker's beak in the woods? You have a magical inner voice. Sometimes it can be as silent as a crocus growing in spring or the fragrance of a rose bathed in sunlight. This voice is full of wisdom. It is always there to answer any query or question you may have. Anyone can hear it but it will only talk to those who are willing to listen.

Now that you have discovered and begun to practise ways of calming your inner chatter you can begin to have a relationship with your inner thoughts that is consistently productive and inspiring. There are many different techniques you can use that will help you to find your quiet inner voice.

The method for finding that inner voice is called 'tuning'. It is a little like finding the perfect pitch as you tune a guitar. You know when you have found it because the sound of a perfect C or D or E feels right. It is also like looking for your favourite radio station. Until you know the exact frequency of the station you find it by trial and error. You use the tuning dial, turning it this way and that until you find the programme you want to listen to. Sometimes even when you do know the frequency, say MW648 for the BBC World Service, the band width may be narrow and you will need to fiddle with the dial to get the strongest signal.

Tuning into anything successfully takes two steps.

- Focus
- Intention

Focus is the ability of being present, in the now. You become totally involved in what you are doing or experiencing and remain undistracted. This is a skill and it takes practice.

I am going to outline a number of exercises based on the practice of meditation for you to experiment with. Try each one and then use the ones that you enjoy best on a regular basis. They should not be a chore. The trick to gaining the most benefit from focusing or meditative exercises is to allow them to work on you rather than trying hard or working at them. I have suggested ways in which you can incorporate them into your daily activities. You should not practise these techniques while using machinery or driving.

Breathing Numbers
Is the basic relaxation exercise which you were introduced to in Chapter 1. You will be well versed with it by now so you can begin to experiment a little. This exercise is so simple and easy that you can do it standing up, sitting down, whilst walking, standing in line, waiting for a bus or in the bath. In fact, any time or place when you have three to five minutes to yourself.

> Keeping your eyes open, simply breathe slowly to a count of four, like so.
> Draw the breath in 1 2 3 4, and gently sigh it out 1 2 3 4
> Breathe deeply in 1 2 3 4, and relax it out 1 2 3 4
> Deeply in 2 3 4, relax out 2 3 4
> Deeply in 2 3 4, relax out 2 3 4
> Deeply in 2 3 4, relax out 2 3 4
> Good. Draw the breath in, relax the breath out
> That's it, just breathe in (pause 2 3 4) and out (pause 2 3 4)
> Continue to breathe rhythmically and as you do notice how tension moves out of your body with each exhalation

Pay attention to the movement of your breath in and out as you count

Continue to breathe this way for five minutes

Walking Breath

You can do this exercise anywhere that you can take 12 paces in a straight line. My personal preference is to leave the house. I will do this exercise while walking to the shops and taking the dog for a run.

Walk a little slower than usual

Use the rhythm of Breathing Numbers to dictate the pace

Now allow your feet to rise and fall to the rhythm of that count

Breathe to the rhythm of your walk

Focus your attention on the rise and fall of your feet

Continue to breathe to the rhythm of your walk as you focus your attention on the rise and fall of your feet

Remain focused on your breath and your feet for five minutes.

This exercise has been tried and tested many times over. To reassure you that your responses are normal here are some examples from past students of the things we would have expected you to notice:

- I had to adjust the speed of my breath to my walking pace until I got it right
- I felt light-headed, but walking and focusing on my feet prevented me from getting dizzy
- Concentrating too hard gave me a headache
- It was really difficult trying to do two things at once
- Afterwards I felt energized, but also quite relaxed
- Focusing on breathing whilst walking to work stopped me from worrying about what the day would bring
- Usually I get very fidgety when I meditate, but being able to move around helped a lot

Breathing Friends

I was introduced to this exercise when I was a student on an NLP course. It is a powerful way to build rapport. It demands a degree of concentration but your efforts will be well rewarded. It certainly has the effect of strengthening emotional bonds and builds trust and intimacy between people. I have found the best way to practise Breathing Friends is to either lay side by side or sit opposite your partner cross-legged or in straight-backed chairs.

Decide which of you will be the passive breather. Your role will be to sit or lie comfortably with closed eyes and breathe normally. It is inappropriate to force your breath in any way. Simply relax and breathe to your natural rhythm.

Decide which of you will be the active breather. Your role is to match and mimic exactly the breathing rhythm of your passive partner. You will breathe as deep, hold the breath as long and exhale exactly as they do and for the same amount of time. Once you have matched your partner's breathing rhythm – this will take approximately eight to ten breaths – you will exhale and release the breath with a gentle sigh like 'ahhh'.

Breathe together like this for five minutes. Then both take a deep breath and blow out hard. Stand and stretch. At this point you may like to change roles and repeat the exercise.

This exercise has been tried and tested many times over. To reassure you that your responses are normal here are some examples from past students of the things we would have expected you to notice:

- I started getting out of breath trying to follow my partner's breathing pace
- It was interesting to learn how the pace of my partner's inhale and exhale was different to my own normal breathing
- Concentrating on someone else required more effort than focusing on myself
- You develop a synchronicity with your partner which is the kind of intimacy you don't get normally just being with someone

Intention is the action of expressing a desire or expecting an outcome while in a state of focus. You will have already experienced the result of intention in the exercise on body focusing in Chapter 4. To jog your memory pay attention to the way your body responds to the passage below. Read it slowly to allow time for the changing sensations to develop.

Take a moment to find the most pleasurable sensation in your body right now. Ask yourself: where can I feel a comfortable and pleasurable sensation in my body right now? Wait for a few seconds. What do you notice? Where is your attention focused at this moment? Now take a deep breath. As you breathe shift your attention. Focus on another part of your body. How has the sensation moved with your thought? You may observe some pleasurable sensation moving to this part of your body as energy follows your thought. Breathe, and know that as your attention shifts, energy moves toward your point of focus.

For the archer it is the focus of vision and the intention of thought
that speeds the arrow to its target

We have found that one of the best and most fun ways to develop your focus and intention muscles is to play. For the following games you can use a variety of objects that you can comfortably throw and catch.

- Play catch by bouncing a ball off a wall – use different sized balls for different effects.
- Stand squarely, your feet slightly apart. Keep your hands 18 inches apart and toss an object from one hand to the other. Use different sized and weighted objects for different effects.
- Learn to juggle – start with something light and easy to grip like bean bags and move on to oranges.
- From 20 paces aim to hit a tree with a pebble. If you miss a lot train yourself by throwing the pebble from 5 paces. Increase the distance one pace at a time until you can hit the tree square on from 20 paces or more.
- Make it into a social affair. Get together with your children and friends and have some fun. Shoot some baskets. Go tenpin bowling. Play baseball, pool, boule, hoops, table tennis and lawn tennis.

Take some time to relax before each game. Remember to breathe and focus. Look at the place where you want the ball to end up. Watch what you are intending to catch and go with the flow.

As you touch this page and feel the paper under your fingertips you can become aware of your hands. And as you read and focus your attention on the words you can still notice how this book feels in your hands. And it may be interesting to know that your mind can be busy absorbing the meaning of the words and you can also be aware of so many other things. And I wonder how many things you can be aware of as you read. You can be aware of so many things and at the same time cannot help but focus your attention on the words you are reading. And as your eyes follow the words you may be aware of the feeling of this book as it rests in your hands. And how does it feel to hold this book as you read the text? Where do you notice the most pressure? Is it on the palm of one hand or on the other or do your fingertips take the weight of these type-filled pages? And as you begin to discover exactly how you hold this book you may notice that you are making some adjustments with your hands and fingers. And how much more comfortably can you hold this book as you read it? And you are reading so many questions. I wonder how curious you can be about the words you will see as your eyes skim across this page. And what will you read next as you notice how your arms adjust to the weight of the book in your hands? What would it be like to read a passage in a book and to find that just by reading your body could begin to relax? And what is it like to discover that even as you read the muscles in your face can relax? And I wonder how you will discover the answer to the questions that you have just read? And you know reading is an interesting skill. You can discover so many things as you read. You can discover many things in the words and you can also discover

things that are not written? And how is it to discover that
you know things that you did not know that you knew?
And I wonder how you will find out? And as you find out
what can you notice? You can notice the pace of your
breathing whilst you sit and read. You can notice how
your thoughts can be here and somewhere else at the
same time. And what thoughts enter your mind whilst you
sit and read? How do your thoughts change as you read
and discover new images in your mind? Every thought you
have can create some image. It may be related to the words
on the page or it could be an image evoked by a thought
that has momentarily passed through your mind. I do not
know what you can see in your mind, but I do know that
you can recognize now that you can be in this room
reading this material, and at the same time be in your own
world of image and sound. Thus simply by running your
eyes over the typeface in front of you, you can integrate so
many ideas and new discoveries and information that can
be of importance in some special way. And later when you
need to remember things of importance you can recall all
the information you need. You already know that time
can seem to stretch and shrink. Have you noticed how
long a kettle takes to boil when you watch it and how fast
time seems to move when you are having fun? Your awareness of time and space is altered with each task that you
have accomplished, and with each accomplishment you
can feel good about the fact that you spent just the right
amount of time on it. Now listen to your breath – take a
deep breath now. Your chest can rise and fall as you
recognize that there has been a change in your level of
relaxation. Your mind may begin to wander as you wonder
what new methods of learning you may have gained from
reading this text. And as you breathe deeply that wondering can help you to integrate any new learning into everyday awareness so that you can discover the many benefits
in your own way. You can begin to find a pleasurable

image for your inner eyes to see. And as you read the words on this page that pleasurable image can become clearer and clearer. And you can have a sense of curiosity about a pleasurable image as it comes more and more to mind. And how does an image like that feel as you notice your breathing? What pleasant sensations can arise from an image like that as you notice a change in your body? And as you notice the sensations can develop with the rhythm of your breath. And you know that your heart beats to a rhythm too. And with the rhythm of each heartbeat a pleasurable sensation can flow deep into your body filling every cell, and as that rhythm flows, it is so very easy to just let go. And what can release from your body with each outward breath. And you can wonder how much benefit you can receive from a rhythmic sensation like that, as it flows through your body in this way as you breathe in and out. And you know what it is like to breathe rhythmically and slowly. And you can discover so many wonderful things with the rise and fall of your chest. And I wonder what you can discover? And how does a sensation like that lead to relaxation? And what kind of a relaxation is a relaxation like that? What level of relaxation have you reached now and how much more deeply will your bodymind choose to relax as you continue to breathe rhythmically in and out? Will it be just a little more or will you relax even further than you have managed to relax before? How will it feel to be as relaxed and as comfortable as you can be? And what kind of comfortable breathing can you do to the count of four? And as you listen I wonder what you might hear in the sound of the rise and fall of your chest? I wonder what there may be as you wonder what you may now hear. And you may now begin to hear a peaceful voice. And as you listen to the sound of your breath, what is a peaceful voice that speaks to you like that? And what kind of a peaceful voice is a peaceful voice like that? And I do not know what your inner peaceful voice might say. But I do know that you can wonder at the wisdom of a peaceful voice that lies within the landscape of your mind. It is a quiet, gentle voice. And when your ears are open you can listen to a quiet, gentle voice inside your mind. You may hear it as the rustle of a breeze or from a bubbling brook or in a bird song. It may be as silent as a bluebell growing in the grass or the fragrance of a rose bathed in sunlight. And you can wonder, is there a message in the soft pitter patter of a raindrop or the tap, tap, tapping of the woodpecker in the woods. And as you listen to the rhythm with inner ears, and remember breathing to a count, you can wonder about a peaceful voice that lives in your mind. And I wonder what is an inner voice like that? And how does a peaceful magical voice that lives within the landscape of your mind converse with your bodymind? And how does your bodymind listen to that voice in its own special way? And you can discover this voice is full of wisdom. And as you discover you may find that a voice that sounds like the rustle of a breeze or a bubbling brook can answer any question you may have. And as you listen to your breath you can remember that a quiet, gentle voice inside your mind will only talk when you are willing to listen. And how does a peaceful voice talk to your bodymind? And how does your bodymind listen to a peaceful voice that it can hear in its own special way? And what kind of an encounter can you have with a peaceful voice that you can see? And what can a peaceful voice look like as it talks with you as you breathe and relax? And as you breathe how can an inner image of a peaceful voice become clearer and clearer? And as you experience an awareness of that peaceful voice, in your own special way, you may encounter that peaceful voice with inner eyes. And now you know that in a peaceful inner voice can be an image for your inner eyes to see and a sound for your inner ears to hear.

And as you finish this paragraph you can find yourself closing your eyes as you take some time to sit quietly and receive a rhythmic light that flows through your body as you breathe. And you can receive all the benefit that you need from a rhythmic light in a very short time. And your mind knows about time and can measure the benefit of five minutes of breathing a bright light. And as you finish this paragraph you can take five minutes to close your eyes and breathe. And your mind knows about time and can measure five minutes and with a quiet inner voice remind you to open your eyes. And when it is time for your eyes to open you can really feel the relief of taking the time to rest and release from your bodymind all that you no longer needed as you come to full waking awareness once again.

Focus on your feet. You can feel the floor beneath you. Now focus on your feet and as you feel them flex and wiggle your toes. Stretch your body. Breathe in deeply and blow out hard as if you were blowing out candles on a birthday cake. Good. Breathe in again and blow out even harder this time. Great. *Now stretch your body and open your eyes*. Look around you. What colours can you see? Clap your hands hard together several times before you continue with your day.

Well done. Put the book to one side for a while.

Now do something completely different.

15   The quiet mind

You are on a journey through life and you have chosen a path to self-fulfilment. The journey is well under way now and some of the territory you have crossed will have been unfamiliar. The Hopi Indians say that the environment affects the man more than man affects the environment. If this is the case you will have been transformed in some way by your journey. You will have discovered many things about yourself. Whilst I have some idea of what you have experienced, only you can discover how this will become part of your life. Realizations, whether profound or superficial, will always lead to a modification in attitude, perspective, behaviour and ultimately in the way that we relate to our environment and others.

Accommodating change, no matter how much it is needed or invited, is always a challenge. Sometimes the effects are subtle and barely noticeable even to those who know us intimately. Then there are those profound moments of clarity, insights that hit the mark with a flash of stark intensity, from which nothing ever looks the same again.

From self-discovery there can be no return to ignorance

During any new or intensive phase of learning there will be a time when you just cannot take in any more information. No matter how hard you try you do not seem able to concentrate or the words and ideas in front of you just do not seem to make any kind of sense. When this occurs you have reached saturation point. It is a natural and inevitable consequence of self-discovery and change. It shows that you are right on track and is a positive sign. It also shows that something marvellous is happening.

A caterpillar calls it the end of the world.
The universe calls it a butterfly.

You may begin to experience panic, fatigue, frustration, boredom, unfamiliar feelings, unexpected emotions, confusion, helplessness and you may even begin to doubt yourself, your friends or the subject you are studying. When you begin to have these kind of feelings it is time to break your journey for a while. Attempting to move on will only exacerbate the problem. This is the point in your travels when you are waiting fogbound in the airport departure lounge for a connecting flight. All planes have been grounded until further notice. There is nothing else to be done but take stock, accept the situation and relax. It is a time of integration.

Integration is a time of gestation. Once you have ploughed the land, fertilized the soil and sown the seeds you must wait until the crops are ready to harvest. Nature has a cycle, you cannot rush it. The crops will take all the time they need to ripen and, given the right conditions, that is exactly what they will do. You can be certain that now these seeds are planted they will grow.

So how do you deal with the symptoms of change? My first suggestion is to break your routine in some way. Take a couple of days off and do something you enjoy. Here are some of my favourites.

- Relaxation and breathing exercises
- Eating out at a favourite restaurant
- Watching *Star Trek* videos
- Baking fudge brownies
- Walking in the woods
- Playing sport
- Relaxing in a steamy fragrant bath
- Drawing or painting whatever comes to mind
- Playing with the children
- Visiting and laughing with friends

I really cannot express too strongly the importance of taking time out. It refreshes the mind, sweeps away the cobwebs, rejuvenates your immune system and gives you time to appreciate life.

> *The world is only tolerable because of the empty places in it –*
> *millions of people all crowded together, fighting and struggling,*
> *behind them, somewhere, enormous, empty places.*
> *I tell you what I think, when the world's filled up, we'll have to get*
> *hold of a star. Any star. Venus, or Mars. Get hold of it and leave*
> *it empty. Man needs an empty space for his spirit to rest in.*
>
> Doris Lessing

Now is a time for resting, so there is no practical exercise in this section. However, to facilitate the integration of any information or ideas that are milling around in your head, please read the Multi Level Reading passage below. Remember to read slowly, pausing for a moment between each sentence. If you have a piece of calming instrumental music that you enjoy please play it now.

You have been reading and you are reading now and listening to the words that your eyes can see. Even as you read the words you may become aware of an inner commentary whilst at the same time being aware of sounds that surround you. As you listen to the words with inner ears you can remember other exercises that you have experienced in this book. And as you remember what do you recall about breathing? And what kind of breathing can you do to the count of four? And as you listen with inner ears and remember breathing to the count of four, you may remember in your own way how a natural breathing rhythm can relax your mind and body. And as you recall what it is like to breathe rhythmically and slowly you will recognize how the rise and fall of your chest can extend these growing sensations of relaxation. And you can read to the rhythm of your breath. And what kind of reading do you do to a breathing rhythm? And how does the pace

of your breathing link to the pace of your reading as you recognize how the rise and fall of your chest can extend these growing sensations of relaxation? And what kind of a relaxation is a relaxation like that? What level of relaxation have you reached now as you read these words and how much more deeply will your bodymind choose to relax as you continue to breathe rhythmically in and out? Will it be just a little more or will you relax even further than you have managed to relax before? How will it feel to be as relaxed and as comfortable as you can be? And what kind of breathing can you do to the count of four? And as you listen to the rhythm with inner ears, and remember breathing to that count, you may also have a memory of choosing a happy thought. And what kind of a happy thought was a happy thought which your mind and body can experience in their own special way? And as you experience those special sensations you can encounter that memory with inner eyes. And what kind of a special encounter is an encounter like that as your inner vision becomes clearer and clearer? (pause here as your inner vision develops)

And now you know you can find an image for your inner eyes to see that becomes clearer and clearer like a blue blue sky on a warm summer day . . . and you can wonder where seeing inner eyes can find a fluffy white cloud in a blue blue sky on a warm summer day. And you can have a sense of curiosity about a fluffy white cloud as your inner eyes see light. And as you breathe, you can wonder how would it feel to breathe light into your body from a fluffy white cloud as it gets closer and closer now . . . And what kind of feeling is a feeling of breathing in light? What pleasant sensations can you notice as you absorb that light into your body? And as you notice the rhythm of your breath, you know that your heart beats to a rhythm too. And with the rhythm of each heartbeat that light can flow deep into your body, filling every cell, and as that light flows, it is so very easy, to just let go of pockets of tension or tightness which leave your body with each outward breath. And you can wonder how much benefit you can receive from a rhythmic light that flows through your body in this way as you breathe in and out. And you can receive all the benefit that you need in a very short time of between two to five minutes. Your mind knows about time and can measure the benefit of five minutes of breathing a bright light and then remind you to open your eyes. And as you finish this paragraph you can find yourself closing your eyes as you take some time to sit quietly and receive a rhythmic light that flows through your body. And when it is time for your eyes to open you can really feel the relief of taking the time to rest and release from your bodymind all that you no longer need as you come to full waking awareness once again.

As you come to full awareness once again focus on your feet. You can feel the floor beneath you. Now focus on your feet and as you feel them flex and wiggle your toes. Stretch your body. Breathe in deeply and blow out hard as if you were blowing out candles on a birthday cake. Good. Breathe in again and blow out even harder this time. Great. *Now stretch your body and open your eyes.* Look around you. What colours can you see? Clap your hands hard together several times before you continue with your day.

Well done. Now take some quality time out for yourself. *Hasta Manana.*

Part 2

16   *Feeling thoughts*

By now, groundwork you put in during Part 1 will be beginning to pay off. You should be feeling more motivated, focused, positive and generally more relaxed. These foundations need to have solidified somewhat before you can successfully advance to the next level, so if you have ignored the advice and not yet taken any time out, please stop reading now and find something else to do for a while. The book will still be here when you get back!

Through the exercises in Chapters 1, 2, 4 and 9, you now know that your mind and body are inextricably linked. Experience has shown you that your thoughts influence not only your body but also feelings and, subsequently, your mood. You know that by focusing your attention you can counteract that chattering mind and choose how and what you think. Well, right now, and for a change, I don't want you to think at all. You heard me right. For the next few moments you can be mindless and when you are mindless you won't want to think of anything at all, especially not a blue triangle.

Well, what happened? Did you see a blue triangle? My guess is yes!

How could it be that you would see something you were asked not to think about? The answer lies in the fact that every time you have a thought, your mind creates an image. (Especially when you are not supposed to have one!) Ponder on this question for a moment. What is your favourite time of year? Now that you have thought about that for a few moments how do you know that it's your favourite time of year? I reckon that you know by the feeling you get as you think about it. Usually, a favourite thing, whether a season, a person or something else, creates a good feeling, or at least a feeling that you would like to experience again and again. Whether you realize it or not, that feeling will be linked to that particular thought; and that thought is linked to a particular series of images. As you thought about what you enjoy you saw an image. Every time you see that image you will simultaneously experience the memory of it.

The image you see in your mind may be fuzzy or sharp, coloured or black and white, a snap shot or a movie. It may seem to be inside your head or somewhere outside your body, close or at a distance. I do not know how you see what you see but I do know that as soon as you see it you will feel it . . .

Humour me for a moment. Let's experiment:

1. Sit comfortably
    Read through the instructions (then, if you like, close your eyes)
    Think of a triangle. (If you can't see one, what can you see?)
    What colour is it? Does it have a background?
    Now notice any feelings or sensations that you have as you look at the triangle
    Write down your experience

2. Now repeat the experiment changing the triangle to the following colours one at a time: Red, Yellow, Orange, Lime Green, Blue, Purple, Brown, Grey
    Look at the different coloured images. Be aware of your feelings and any sensations.
    Write down what happened
    Which colours did you enjoy the most? What made them enjoyable?
    Which colours did you dislike? What was your experience of these?

Here are the results that other people achieved:

Harriet

1. A neon turquoise isosceles triangle on a dark blue background. It made my heart feel as if it was flipping over and my throat felt as if it was UFO-shaped.
2. *Red*: I felt a tightness in my chest and got hot and claustrophobic.
   Yellow: Felt automatically happy – expansive sensations around my heart and head.
   Orange: Felt comforting and earthy. Pulling, grounding sensations like a half-moon shape in my lower back.
   Lime Green: Felt exhilarated, like running fast over green fields.
   Blue: I feel serene and peaceful. It was like being in a secluded open place watching the sky.
   Purple: Felt calm and serene. Aware of cartwheeling sensations above my head.
   Brown: It is in my belly. It feels disturbing, like when I have a negative thought.
   Grey: Feels like a thick foggy cloud around me that I can't get out of.
   Enjoyed: Yellow, Lime Green, Orange, Purple because of the expansive sensations in different parts of my body.
   Disliked: Brown and Grey. My face automatically screws up! Red almost made me panic!
   Comments: I did not know that my body was so influenced by my imagination. I realize now that I can change my mood just by changing an image in my mind.

Thea

1. A crystal isosceles triangle with clouds and sky moving within it on an intense dark blue, almost black background. There were expansive feelings in my tummy and a kind of wonder.
2. *Red*: A red pyramid appears quite a long way away on a darker background. Feels curious.

Yellow: An isosceles triangle in a field of sunflowers against a blue sky. Feels like a doorway into something happy.

Orange: I'm in it! There are sounds of laughter and pleasure. Feelings of joy.

Lime Green: A triangle lying flat pointing towards my forehead, moving around, spinning and rotating around a computer screen. Feels exciting and exhilarating.

Blue: An electric-blue equilateral triangle right against my forehead with a sky-blue background. I feel as if I'm patiently waiting for something.

Purple: A pyramid above and in front of my head which appears to be full of moving purple water with light reflecting off it. It has a silver base. Feels mentally expansive and full of spiritual information.

Brown: A chestnut wooden pyramid on grass with trees behind it. Feels centring, grounding, commanding and very present.

Grey: A tetrahedron in front and to the right. Feels like a war memorial, sombre and intense.

Enjoyed: Orange, Brown and Purple because these had the strongest physical sensations – powerful, intense and real.

Disliked: Didn't dislike any, but the least interesting was the Blue because it was waiting. Nothing to see other than colour and nothing was happening.

Comments: I was amazed by the responses. They were so detailed and vivid. I didn't know I could do this! I want to find out how to best use this skill.

Just to reassure you that whatever you experienced was absolutely appropriate for you; in the ten years that I have been using this exercise, no two people have ever seen exactly the same triangle or had the same response to the colours. Contrary to popular belief it appears that:

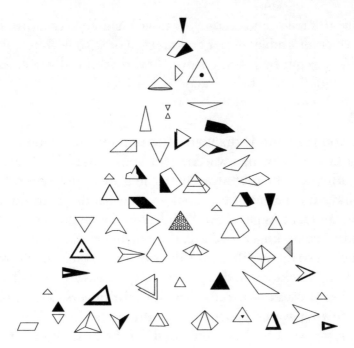

Great minds do not think alike!

And what can we learn from this experiment? Well . . .

- The mind doesn't always follow your instructions verbatim
- Colour can influence mood
- Imagination plays an important and powerful role in changing your state
- We are influenced by the pictures in our minds
- We are not at the mercy of our thoughts
- We can choose how we feel
- Mind and body are inextricably linked
- This can be a powerful resource for healing and change
- An image can evoke an experience of feeling/emotion/ sensation (We will discuss the implications of this later)

And now another reading exercise which will help you to develop the bodymind by fine-tuning your capacity for feeling images. You can gain some benefit from reading this slowly and you can gain a different benefit by committing the following passage to tape then listening to it with closed eyes. Now, make yourself comfortable, either cross-legged or with both feet flat on the floor. Begin by reading slowly and rhythmically. Remember to pause for breath at the end of each sentence.

As you read and focus your attention on these words you can have a growing awareness of your hands. With every breath you take that awareness can grow. How will it feel to have the weight of this book in your hands? Your finger-tips can feel this page? And while you notice the sensations under your fingers you can remember that you have touched so many different things before. You know how it feels to stroke something soft. It is so easy to recall the feeling of water as it runs through your fingers. The sound of flowing water can be so soothing, can't it? You can really appreciate that your mind can be busy doing many different things at once. You can read and simultaneously sense your surroundings. You can hold something in your hands and breathe. You can relax and have a pleasant memory. So, you can be aware of all these things and simultaneously focus some of your attention on these words. And as your eyes follow them you may wonder if I will ask you to breathe in a rhythmic way? Wouldn't it be curious to discover that you could breathe like that without making a conscious effort to do so? Could it be that you have counted 1, 2, 3, 4 so many times before that your body knows exactly what to do when you see that number sequence 1, 2, 3, 4. You know as you relax your body automatically makes some adjustments. As you increase your level of comfort you can count and change the pace of your breathing. How much better can you feel just by counting 1, 2, 3, 4? Now, you can observe how your breath deepens in a rhythmic way and be curious to discover within you an ocean of calmness. The sound of waves lapping on a sandy beach can be so restful. And this ocean of calmness can become a feeling that will spread throughout your body in its own particular way. How does it feel to now be gaining a sense of calmness within you? I wonder when that calmness will flow through your mind. How will it be to experience a growing sense of peace and calm throughout your bodymind? And as you experience the peace and serenity of those flowing sensations, how best can you notice a growing sense of balance and harmony? This ocean can sway and swell as you breathe and read, and soon you will see that you can be as peaceful as the motion of waves in calm weather.

Now there is deep within your unconscious awareness a centre core. You may be aware of it from time to time as it has been there with you since the time you were a little child. Sometimes it is an inner guide or counsel. It may be a 'higher self' or 'guardian angel'. Now I cannot tell what it can be for you, but you will soon find out. I wonder what you might discover as you recognize a peaceful inner voice that you have heard before. Now relax and rest in the motion of your deep and rolling ocean and listen for it now. And as you discover this special voice you can just take another breath and wonder how deeply you can relax. How deeply can that be as you flow safely to that inner core? And what is the best that it can be? You can discover in your own way that this core can guide you from within. So, by your own inner guidance you can now continue to find your way toward your destination. You know deep inside you what that destination will be, and can it be that you can experience the feelings of being there now in a similar way that you experience this ocean of calmness? Perhaps it will be that way or maybe some other? How can a destination become a feeling that spreads throughout your bodymind in its own distinctive way? How will it feel to know you are gaining the momentum to move forward? What would it be like to grow stronger and stronger every day? I wonder how those qualities will flow through your mind. What would it be like to experience a growing sense of self-awareness and self-respect with every breath you take? Now you can have a developing experience in a peaceful and balanced way, as those feelings flow, synchronizing your mind and body in this particular way. So, what is it like to have a special growing state of harmony, peace and balance as you breathe and read and watch it grow so that you have exactly what you need?

You have the capacity to see yourself in the future. You can find a pleasurable image for your inner eyes to see. You know that as you read an image like that can become clearer and clearer. What is it like to be curious about living up to your dreams? And how does it feel to see an image like that as you notice your breathing? What pleasant sensations can arise from that image as you notice a change in your body? It can be easy to notice new sensations that develop with the rhythm of your breath. Your heart beats to a rhythm too. You can be certain with each heartbeat a pleasurable sensation can flow throughout your body, filling every cell, and as that rhythm flows, it is so very easy to immerse yourself in an ocean of internal harmony, peace and balance as you let go and make space in your life to experience new things. What is the best thing you can release from your body with each outward breath to make room for those special new feelings? You may continue to see yourself living well in the future. As you walk into it one step at a time you can know that your unconscious mind, your deep inner core will be there whenever you need it. It can guide you like an internal coach. What would it be like to have an inner guide with a special inner voice that can guide you by instinct and intuition and wisdom even as you sleep? And you can take all the time you need to find out.

And as you finish this paragraph you may find yourself closing your eyes for a few moments. You may choose to take some time to sit quietly and receive a rhythmic light that flows through your body like a peaceful voice as you breathe. When it is time for your eyes to open you will know and come to full waking awareness once again.

As your eyes open you can focus on your feet. You can feel the floor beneath you. Now focus on your feet and as you feel them flex and wiggle your toes. Stretch your body. Breathe in deeply and blow out hard. And again breathe deeply in and blow out hard. Be ready to *stretch your body and look around you*. What colours can you see? What kind of an experience was that? Well done. Now do something physical like washing the dishes or walking the dog.

17   *Food for thought*

Communication is fundamental to our existence. Take a walk in nature and you will surely be surrounded by an orgy of sound and colour and signals designed to communicate something about the evolution of species (usually about territory, sex or food). To guarantee success the signal needs to be specific, direct, noisy, fragrant and very attractive. A little like advertising!

Think about those triangles for a moment. Easy, isn't it? I wonder why that is? Could imagination have something to do with it? I wonder whether colour and shape with all its complex variety may communicate some deep meaning that we have consciously (and inconveniently) forgotten. Why would we respond both physically and emotionally to something that we do not consciously understand? The answer may come from the time shortly after you were born. At that time you could not think or reason or question because you had no language. Without language you cannot think. After all, thinking is listening to words inside your head.

There you were a tiny, helpless, human being aware only of the fact that your environment had changed and that you were

hungry. Instinctively you found a voice which you could flex and add to the other unrecognizable sounds around you. You were held, it was warm. You were fed, there was comfort. You slept. Each time you cried a blurred image appeared in front of your unfocused eyes. It had a soothing sound and smelt of something that you came to recognize as dinner. Then, as sure as night follows day, the sounds, colours, tastes, smells, sensations and images that saturated your world began to take on meaning. That initial understanding of the world still influences you today. It is the rhetoric of your emotion and the alphabet that shapes the words of your inner mind. Thus from meagre beginnings the complexities of language and metaphor are formed.

If a picture paints a thousand words, metaphor gives it meaning

We talk in images:

He's losing his marbles. It's raining cats and dogs.
That's water under the bridge. It's a hot potato.
That's a load of rubbish! Turn over a new leaf.
They've got me over a barrel. The key to success.
They get on like a house on fire. Spill the beans.
I'm green with envy. I'm at the end of my tether.
Never look a gift horse in the mouth.
He saw stars. It's a piece of cake! I've got the needle.
Let's run that up the flagpole and see who salutes!
That takes the biscuit! I'll dance to my own tune.
Don't count your chickens until they hatch.
That's right up my street. She's got a bun in the oven.
I'm at a loose end. I'm a bit tied up at the moment.
Like a bull in a china shop. It's not my cup of tea.
He was so blue. Everything's coming up roses!
Fresh as a daisy. Butter wouldn't melt in her mouth.
He's out of the woods. It keeps the wolf from the door.
That was a close shave! She's got a screw loose.
I'm going round the bend. I'm really browned off.
She's too big for her boots! Don't rock the boat.

You're all mouth and no trousers!   She saw red.
The grass is always greener on the other side.
Wake up and smell the coffee!   Surf the Net.
He went away with his tail between his legs.
There are plenty more fish in the sea. It's a red herring.
You can't pull the wool over my eyes.
She kicked the bucket. That's a pretty kettle of fish!
Let's get down to brass tacks.   She's so two faced!
The world is your oyster. It's all swings and roundabouts.
I've got a bone to pick with you.   And pigs might fly!

Some images have a universal meaning we can all relate to:

Some are religious:

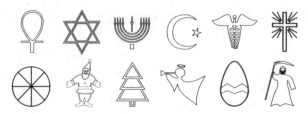

Others indicate a collective identity, interest or kinship:

Metaphor is not necessarily visual. A composer can describe an
idea in the form of a symphony. Think of Holst and his

impression of our solar system – *The Planets*. Then there is Prokofiev's *Peter and the Wolf* and Handel's *Water Music*. Music is a wonderful medium for representing and expressing emotion. Beethoven's *Moonlight Sonata* is a delightful example. What about anthems? They are designed to promote a sense of national pride and identity. What about the movies? Can you imagine The *Big Country*, *Star Wars*, *Chariots of Fire*, *Dances with Wolves*, or *Forrest Gump* without their evocative scores?

Then there was music for a generation that wanted to forge a new identity and break free from past traditions: Rock 'n' Roll, Elvis, The Beatles, Flower Power, Rhythm and Blues, Soul, High Energy, Punk, Modern Romance, Rap, Acid House, Hip Hop, Indie . . . the list is endless.

Metaphor builds bridges between ideas that may have no logical or apparent connection. They help us to express and understand, an unusual or innovative concept or idea in a meaningful way. In English folklore we related animals to different emotional qualities. We still use them in everyday language. We will often hear people say greedy as a pig, courageous as a lion, sly as a fox, stubborn as a mule, hungry as a wolf, wise as an owl, curious as a cat, cheeky as a monkey.

Native American culture has a deep respect and understanding of the natural word. As animals live in a state of equilibrium with nature it is felt that we can learn much by observing their ways. Each animal is assigned a metaphorical quality that matches its lifestyle and behaviour. When emulated it is believed that this knowledge can lead us toward a more balanced and contented life.

BEAR – seeks to find truth through solitude and introspection.

WOLF – loyal and responsible teacher, brings new and intuitive ideas to the clan.

DOG – a guardian and protector unswerving in loyalty and devotion to others.

DOLPHIN – connected to the divine, he represents the life force, teaches us how to release emotions through sacred breath.

SNAKE – the power of creation through sexual and psychic energy, the universal force of transmutation is embodied here.

EAGLE – learns from life's ups and downs to conquer fear by rising above the mundane into the realms of the Great Spirit.

Sometimes the links we make are accidental. At other times through advertising they are contrived like Coke and children singing all over the world. Who could have imagined that millions of people would discover an appreciation of opera while watching football. Now Pavarotti and the World Cup are synonymous. What does a famous brand of lager, the theme from *Mission Impossible* and a squirrel have in common? Some links are made which are dependent on whether you live in a country or are a visitor. Think about Big Ben and London, the Statue of Liberty and New York and the Taj Mahal and India. Are the links we make ever purely accidental? As well as social and cultural connections you will also have made links between things that have specific meaning to you. These are often of a personal or intimate nature and can bring into play your sense of smell. Think of newly-cut grass for instance, freshly-baked bread, roast turkey, honeysuckle, jasmine and roses, or a fragrance that someone special to you wears.

Carry a pen and a pad with you for the next few days. As you remember or notice how you connect things together, make a list. This will exercise your memory and your emotions. If you should come across anything unpleasant go to Chapter 11 and read the Multi Level Reading exercise.

And now another reading exercise which will help you to integrate these concepts of language and image. You can gain some benefit from reading this slowly and you can gain a different benefit by committing the following passage to tape then listening to it with closed eyes. Now, make yourself comfortable, either cross-legged or with both feet flat on the floor. Begin by reading slowly and rhythmically. Remember to read pausing for a moment between each sentence. If you have a piece of calming instrumental music that you enjoy please play it now.

You already know that your mind knows where it stores all your memories. So because your mind knows these things you can easily re-experience any memory that makes you feel so good. Now where in your mind could you discover a pleasant, pleasing memory? And as you can find out, in what way will you allow those sensations to expand and grow? With each moment you can keep on feeling better and better. So, you might wonder in your own unique way just how much better that can be? Just how good can you really feel as your eyes follow the text on this page? Will the feelings continue to grow with each

word you read or will those feelings peak in a short while? Only you can discover the answer as you read and breathe in a growing relaxed and comfortable way. Now you may begin to be curious about some special moments in your life as these good feelings develop even more. You can learn so much when you are curious. You are learning now that self-discovery is so very easy. And what can you discover next? What could be the most effortless way to learn something good about yourself? As you get to know more about the places in your mind where you have good memories you can begin to recall a time when learning something was very easy. How easy it is to feel that learning can be an exciting experience. You have been learning by reading words on this page. Once more, as you listen to your breath, how will you remember all those times when you have learnt with no effort at all? And a memory can come to mind in a moment and it can also take a few moments to come to mind.

You have all the time you need and I wonder what you need to know? So, how will you find out? You know that words are formed from letters. Each letter represents a sound, doesn't it? Now, I wonder how you learnt those sounds? It was probably a long time ago, and you learnt that words can be sounds that we make when we want to be understood. You can understand them as you read. And as you read you can understand many other things that are new to you. When you read you can hear in-formation that you see. As you hear with inner ears you understand. And some things you do not understand, and maybe you don't need to understand everything?

As you allow all these realizations to become one you in-hale and relax. Relaxation and comfort are often synony-mous. It is comfortable to know that a learning from the past can teach you so much in the present? I wonder what kind of present you can have? It is good to be surprised from time to time. What kind of pleasant surprises do you enjoy the most? As you decide you can be comfortable knowing that your relaxation can go even deeper in its own special way. And it is good to discover that your mind is a vast place in which you can store many things. You are just beginning to realize in what way your wonderful mind can support you. And what form can that support take? As your inner mind decides you can find yourself wondering how you will continue to benefit as you begin to come to full waking awareness.

Take a deep breath now as you read the words on this page. Allow the words to focus your attention. You can be present now. And as you finish this paragraph you can choose to close your eyes and breathe in a restful rhythmic way for a few moments as you gather yourself together. Take some time and sit quietly to integrate any new information and ideas in this chapter. When it is time for your eyes to open you will know that it is so easy to learn and understand things easily.

Now breathe and focus on your feet. You can feel the floor beneath you. Now focus on your feet and as you feel them flex and wiggle your toes. Stretch your body. Breathe in deeply and blow out hard. And again breathe deeply in and blow out hard. Be ready to *stretch your body and open your eyes*. Look around you. What colours can you see? Clap your hands several times. That was an illuminating experience. Well done. Now do something physical like washing the dishes or walking the dog.

18 Trust

Storytime

Some years ago I was in love with a young man from Munich. Al and I met in a London pub where he was attempting to learn the English language by immersing himself in the beer. In his free time he worked as a clerk in a shipping office. After a balmy summer catching the sun by the side of a makeshift football pitch in Regent's Park we planned a trip to Germany. My grandmother was against it. Polish by birth, she still remembered her terror as a goose-stepping army invaded her homeland. The anguished stories of a starving ghetto existence that still haunted her etched in my mind a colourless, surreal image of the country and the people I was about to meet.

Our journey, designed to get us from one port of call to our destination as quickly as possible, still took many hours. We crossed the Channel and rolled off the ferry near beaches where men had died. We drove across Belgium and through France. I wondered how it would have looked from the inside of a tank. Slowly the miles of ever-changing landscape swept away my grandmother's blinding images. I could see peace and beauty in the rolling fields and open sky. I could breathe once again.

We arrived at a white-fronted town house. Al was excited to be home while I was tired and disoriented by the long journey and unfamiliar surroundings. The door was opened by welcoming hands which grasped mine firmly in greeting. I felt uncertain and uncomfortable as I entered the domain of this noisy family. I was an honoured guest, isolated by my own ignorance of a language I didn't understand. My grandmother's voice called to me. For a moment I was drawn back into a time of which I had no memory, yet was not allowed to forget. I felt alone.

A woman's hand touched my arm for a moment. 'Follow me' she motioned. I nodded uneasily and was led into the kitchen. She smiled. In a second I was offered a drink. Suddenly I was playing a spontaneous game of charades rich in laughter, mime and gesture. The prize was a mug of steaming black coffee, aromatic and sweet, caressing my throat. Al was still nowhere to be found – desperately I wondered what might be the gesture for 'bathroom'!

To diminish fear, develop trust in your ability to handle anything

It has been said that life is the greatest teacher. We learn by experience and experience leaves an imprint. We call these imprints memories and they are stored in our minds like reference books in a library. We all have our favourite books, some have stories full of adventure and daring, others can be brimming with cautionary tales.

As we seek solutions and strategies for dealing with the challenges of this Herculean adventure called 'Life on Planet Earth' we will search through our internal library to find them. Sometimes answers can be found in a book we pick up often. We know the words well and may hear familiar and reassuring voices in our mind. The instructions are standard, predictable, easy to follow and we always 'get a result'. We like results so we may turn the instructions into rules and then apply them to every situation we come across. These rules can be advantageous or restrictive.

Predictably, there will be times when you find yourself covering new ground. You may be in unfamiliar territory and there is no map to follow. When we approach the unknown, familiar inner voices can become particularly noisy. They can fill your mind with information based on past experience. This may be the only reference point you have and it may, or may not, be appropriate to the situation you are facing now. When making decisions it can seem hard to ignore those safe, familiar inner voices full of fearful anticipation. The familiar, whether helpful or downright obstructive, can still feel much safer than the unknown. *Here* is, after all, still more familiar than *there*. Under these circumstances how do you get by and have the situation work for you? What do you do when your rules don't apply?

> *He who knows others is wise, he who knows himself is enlightened*
> Lao Tzu

Here is the dictionary definition of trust.

> trust I n. firm belief that a person or thing may be relied upon; state of being relied upon; confident expectation

This is what your emotional coach considers it to be.

> trust is . . . the antidote to uncertainty
> trust is . . . the ability to doubt fear
> trust is . . . possibility
> trust is . . . losing the need to know exactly what the future holds
> trust is . . . a state of curiosity and openness
> trust is . . . opportunity
> trust is . . . belief in yourself

Here are some guidelines to help you incorporate the above ideas into your life:

- **Relax** – You know how. Breathe in 2, 3, 4 and out 2, 3, 4. And again . . . and again . . . there will always be enough air!
- **Focus** – Be in the present. Ask yourself, 'How does this feel?'
- **Be spontaneous** – Life is an experiment where you get to try on a lot of clothes, you never know what might suit you.
- **Make your own luck** – The future is going to be there whether you are ready for it or not. Take advantage of new situations and the opportunities they offer.
- **Be positive** – Don't tell me what you can't do, show me what you can. Remember if you've learnt one skill you can learn another!
- **Be aware of your objective** – Ask yourself, 'Where am I headed?' You may be surprised at the answer.

- **Be responsible** – You are the captain of your own ship. Who has the rudder?
- **Suspend judgement** – In every situation there is a benefit, you may have to look for it however.

> *If we did all the things we were capable of doing, we would totally astonish ourselves*

And now another reading exercise. I wonder what the benefit will be this time?

Now, make yourself comfortable, either cross-legged or with both feet flat on the floor. Remember to read slowly and rhythmically. Pause for breath at the end of each sentence.

You have been reading now and listening to the words that your eyes can see. Even as you read the words you may become aware of an inner commentary whilst at the same time being aware of sounds that surround you. As you listen to the words with inner ears you can remember other exercises that you have experienced in this book. And what do you recall about breathing? And what kind of breathing can you do to the count of four? You may remember in your own way how a natural breathing rhythm can relax your mind and body. And as you recall what it is like to breathe rhythmically and slowly you will recognize how the rise and fall of your chest can extend these growing sensations of relaxation. How does your relaxation evolve? And what kind of a relaxation is a relaxation like that? What level of relaxation have you reached now and how much more deeply will your bodymind choose to relax as you continue to breathe rhythmically in and out? Will it be just a little more or will you relax even further than you have managed to relax before? How will it feel to be reading and be as comfortable as you can be? And what is it like to breathe like that? You can listen to the rhythm with inner ears, and

remember the sensation of breathing to the count of four. Breathing to that count, you may also have a memory of each and every breath you have drawn into your body. And is it not true that each time you draw breath there is air for you to breathe? And your inner mind is so certain that every time you draw breath there is air to breathe that you never think about it. And your inner mind knows that you can trust that there will always be air to breathe. What would it be like to always breathe deeply? How much trust can you receive from a deep breath? And what kind of breath releases tension as it draws air in? And now your body can trust that each breath can release tension as it needs to. And your body is so certain that it can release tension as it breathes that it does not need to be concerned with it any longer. And what kind of thought can replace a thought that you do not need to think about? How comfortable you can be as each breath increases your comfort. And how does comfort feel as it moves throughout your body? And as your body seeks to discover how comfortable it can become you can trust the developing sensations. And what kind of trust is a trust like that? And your mind and body can experience a trust like that in their own special way. And as you have that special experience you can wonder how you can re-experience it whenever you need to. And just ponder on that thought, just as there is always air to breathe, your inner knowing knows exactly what can happen next. And what is the best thing that can happen when you trust? And now your inner mind can find a way for you to know. You can see with inner eyes and hear with inner ears and have feelings that become clearer and clearer in just the right way. And you can have a sense of curiosity about the best thing that can happen when you trust. And as you breathe and wonder you may remember how it feels to breathe light into your body from a fluffy white cloud. And as you become more and more curious the memory of that cloud gets closer and closer now . . . And what kind of feeling is a feeling of breathing in light from a fluffy white cloud? What pleasant sensations can you notice as you absorb that light into your body? And as you notice the rhythm of your breath you know that your heart beats to a rhythm too. And with the rhythm of each heartbeat that light can flow deep into your body filling every cell, and as that light flows you can trust the benefit of pleasant sensations. And as you have that special experience you can wonder how soon that experience will grow into a new understanding. And a light flows through your body as you breathe in and out. And that understanding can bear fruit as it takes the time to ripen. And I wonder just how large the harvest will be?

And as your eyes come to the end of this paragraph you can find yourself closing your eyes. Now take some time to sit quietly as your inner mind directs your attention to your feet. Remember your feet? They are attached to your ankles. Your feet have toes and as you think of toes you can remember that toes can move up and down. They can curl and straighten. And your body will know when it is time for your eyes to open and you can stand on your feet and feel the ground beneath them as you come to full waking awareness once again.

Focus on your feet and feel the floor beneath you. Flex your ankles and wiggle your toes. Stretch your body. Breathe in deeply and blow our hard. And again breathe deeply in and blow out hard. Be ready to *stretch your body and open your eyes*. Well done. Look around you. What colours can you see? You can trust the ground beneath your feet when you stand. Now do something physical like washing the dishes or the dog.

19 Sanctuary

Your imagination is powerful. It is a tool that when left untamed can destroy your peace of mind with its constant forays into the darker unexplored territory of your mind. In this chapter you are going to harness its spirit, and train this power. No longer will you be at the mercy of a wild mind harried by frequent worries and woes. Imagination when used to its best advantage can make an enormous difference to the quality of your life. The technique you use to tame your imagination is called Creative Visualization. Creative Visualization will teach your imagination how to stay focused while it follows a series of instructions.

OK, let's begin. In order to visualize you simply think of something. Let's try a tree. When you think of a tree what do you see? This is the first one that came to mind for me.

Then this

and this

What about you? What kind of tree can you see? If one doesn't appear immediately don't worry. An image can take a few seconds to materialize. Also it is unlikely that your tree will look exactly like mine. When visualizing everyone 'sees' in a different way. Do not make the mistake of believing that if you can't 'see' clearly with inner eyes that you can't visualize. Very few people can close their eyes and 'see' crystal-clear images. Most have a foggy picture or a vague impression of something being there.

Sometimes nothing appears at all and you may just have a sense of a scene or item that has been described. Another interesting thing about visualizing is that the more outlandish and out of this world you let your imagination be the easier it will be for you to 'see' and remember. Let's experiment. Take a tree and give it a happy smiling face. Now have the tree sing. It could sing opera, jazz, rock 'n' roll if you like. Decorate your tree accordingly. Hang or tie things around the trunk and onto the branches. OK, I am certain that it was easier this time. You can keep that tree or change it or delete it as you wish. However, whatever happens, I'm sure you won't forget it in a hurry.

A sanctuary is a secret refuge that you can find within the realms of your bodymind. You reach it by relaxing, focusing and activating your imagination. In this instance you are going to create a haven in your mind where you can go to get away from the demands of your life. You can use it when you need to relax, take time out, make decisions, experiment with new ideas or behaviour, gather your resources together and play. It is a really useful place to visit during times of stress, when you are studying for exams, or healing after injury, illness or loss of any kind. My sanctuary has become so peaceful over the years that I have made a daily visit a part of my meditation practice.

Your sanctuary can appear to be anywhere, or everywhere. You might discover it on a hillside, or in a desert. It can be out in space or under water, in a jungle or a busy city centre. It can be any shape and any size. It may be a shanty, a palace, a cave or a sacred place in nature with the stars for a roof or a combination of any or all the above. The possibilities are endless and limitless.

As a way of introduction I have put together a vague design. Do not feel that you have to comply with my ideas. Once you get there you can, and probably will, make as many alterations as you like. Here are one or two basic rules you will need to follow.

Every sanctuary has a place for rest and recuperation, a place to play, a place for healing and a place that is sacred. This sacred space is for meditating, praying, listening to your inner voice and for seeking help and advice. Other than these basic criteria the content and decor is up to you. You may, and I am certain that you will, fill it with all the creature comforts and mod cons that you desire to make the time you spend there as pleasurable as you wish.

Your Sanctuary is a private place. Entry is restricted to you. You may have a secret entrance, a doorway that opens to a password like 'open sesame' or any other means to keep your haven exclusive. Entry by others is by invitation only. One client has adopted the Starship Enterprise and simply beams people aboard. Whenever he wants to experiment with a new behaviour he goes to the hollodeck, creates a scenario, chooses a new identity and literally tries it on for size.

Find somewhere comfortable to sit.

> Close your eyes and simply breathe slowly to a count of four
> Draw the breath in 1 2 3 4, and gently sigh it out 1 2 3 4
> Breathe deeply in 1 2 3 4, and relax it out 1 2 3 4
> Deeply in 2 3 4, relax out 2 3 4
> Deeply in 2 3 4, relax out 2 3 4
> Deeply in 2 3 4, relax out 2 3 4
> Good. Draw the breath in, relax the breath out
> That's it. Just breathe in (pause 2 3 4) and out (pause 2 3 4)
> Again (pause for a count of 7)

Now continue to breathe slowly and pay attention to the movement of your breath in and out. Allow your breath to even out at a level that is perfect for you. Just sit still and observe your breath for a few seconds. Notice how your breath can enliven and relax your body as you sit. You only need your breath and a heartbeat to refresh, unwind and focus. That's really fine. It is natural that when you sit quietly in this way that you will have thoughts. When a thought comes to mind allow it to drift. Attend only to your breath. Focus only on the passage of your breath. Now continue to sit quietly and breathe in this manner for five minutes.

OK, that's fine. Now take a very deep breath, sigh and breath out hard. Again, take a very deep breath, blow out hard. Take a very deep breath and then blow out hard. Breathe in. Stretch your arms and shoulders. Open your eyes, breathe out.

Well done. Observing your breathing will have calmed and focused your mind. That completes the preparation for Creative Visualization. You are now going to use your imagination to take a walk in nature. Remember that whatever you see will be absolutely appropriate for you. There are no right or wrongs. Remember to be curious, this is your first lesson and the first time you do anything is often the most exciting. I am sure that you can experience this exercise as you read it, after all, you do 'see' what you think! However, you may get a deeper sense of focus and more vivid pictures with your eyes closed, therefore I recommend that you read it through once and then either commit it to tape or get a friend to read it to you whilst you listen with closed eyes.

You will experience your sanctuary through all your senses as you respond to your imagination.

- Auditory, heard with inner ears
- Visual, seen with inner eyes
- Kinaesthetic, felt or sensed within or around your body
- Olfactory and gustatory responses are unusual but not unheard of!

You may:

- Take on another identity
- Meet a guide or teacher either in animal or human form
- Find yourself in another time

You can have:

- Memories of events you have directly experienced – these are likely to hold information useful to your current issue. The meaning may be literal or metaphoric.

- Memories in the form of metaphor which can take on a historic or futuristic identity.

NB For future reference. Sometimes the experiences you have in your metascape (inner landscape) can be so realistic that you may feel that you have actually lived through, or will be living a scenario. Personally I have very clear convictions about the survival of spirit and I have seen evidence both for and against reincarnation. We do not yet fully understand the nature of the mind or of consciousness. It is not my intention to influence you on this subject. You already have your own ideas and beliefs, and as time goes by they may change one way or the other. My advice is to work with the information you receive. Remember whatever you discover, you are who you are now. A conscious, breathing, alive human being living at the tail end of the twentieth century. When you are not working at self-improvement exercises be focused in the day and remember to enjoy life.

Now adjust your body, make yourself comfortable and take the following paragraphs slowly.

Your imagination is a wonderful commodity. With it you can create things that you have never before dreamed of – simply by thinking. Now cast your mind to a place in nature that you can enjoy. What would it be like to be walking towards a sunrise in a beautiful place like this? As you walk be aware of the environment. Allow any images that come to mind some time to develop. You may find that with every step you take your surroundings can become clearer and clearer. Be aware of your feet as they walk across the ground. Look down at your feet now and notice what type of ground you are walking on? Are you wearing shoes or are you barefoot? What is the texture and feel of the ground under your feet? Just allow each step that you take to enhance your experience in some way that is exactly right for you.

And as you walk you can look around. What can you notice about your surroundings as the sun rises? How does the sky look now? What is the quality of light? Can you notice how the colours are changing? How do the shadows alter as the sun begins to peer over the horizon? And as you watch what can you hear? As you listen you may want to allow some natural sounds to come into the environment. What are you aware of? What can you hear and from which direction is the sound coming from? How do you hear it as the image develops in your mind?

Have you been in a place like this before? Is it somewhere you have been, somewhere you remember, or has your imagination drawn it from your mind?

And as you wander through this pleasing place is there some fragrance that you notice in the air as you walk towards the horizon? You can just keep walking and as your feet tread the ground you can talk to yourself about all the things that you notice in a way that enhances your connection with this place. And I wonder what you can see as you notice the sky above you and the earth beneath your feet? As you walk, and observe, and discover, your eyes can be drawn to something beginning to take shape on the horizon. It is a shape that lies somewhere between you and the rising sun. You can begin to notice a sense of connection as if the shape were calling to you in some way. What thoughts cross your mind as you find yourself walking toward your destination?

As you get closer now you can see that the shape is forming into a building. What kind of a building can you see forming over there? And as you watch, your thoughts may wander as you ask, 'Can this be the sanctuary I have been seeking?' And as you move towards it the surrounding shadows stretch by the light of a rising sun. As you get closer you can begin to notice the sound of water and the air may take on a pleasing perfume that draws you closer still to this magical place. You breathe in the atmosphere as you sense the growing peace and charm of this beautiful terrain, and with a sense of pleasure and wonder you begin to explore your new domain. The sound of water can become stronger now and shortly you will come across a shallow river that is fed by a small waterfall. You will find that you are absolutely alone. The water can become more and more inviting as you watch it and you can choose to remove your garments and slip under the refreshing shower as you wish. How does the water feel against your skin as droplets dripping from your body shimmer like silver as the light reflects off it. You can take as much time as you like to enjoy this place. When you feel cleansed and refreshed you can step out and find all your cares and woes evaporating as the sun dries your skin.

Feeling more relaxed and content now, you look around you. You will soon notice an opening in the rocks near the waterfall. I wonder where it might lead? You may be curious now as you walk towards it. It seems large enough to pass through and you can move through and wonder what could be on the other side. As your eyes adjust to the change in light you find yourself in a cavern. What does it look like? Is it decorated in any way? How does it smell? What about the floor, is it rocky or sandy? There is so much to notice here and as you explore this secluded place somewhere in the shadows you will find a table. As you get closer, you notice something resting upon it. It is just the right size to fit in the palm of your hand. It is a very special and unique kind of gift that someone has left there for you and only you. You can pick it up. You put out your hands to touch it and as your fingertips brush over its surface it slowly dawns on you that this gift has the ability to help you understand many things. You now know that if you hold this gift and focus on a question, that somehow you will receive an answer.

Now you already know that there are many kinds of messages and the best way to find out what they have to say, is to be quiet and listen. So you begin to look for somewhere to sit and rest. You can put the gift into a pocket or pouch and discover how to use it later. You look around the cavern again and you notice a muted glow somewhere over there. It is another opening which will lead you to a stairway and guide you up toward the source of light. At the top of the staircase there is an entrance beyond which you will find another room. You can begin to climb it and you can climb until you reach the top.

You develop a sense that you will find a very special room and you are not disappointed by what you discover. The room is filled with a soft rosy pink light and right in the middle of the floor you notice a comfy seat. You can move toward it and sit down. As you do so a beam of light floods the wall in front of you as if it were a screen. You begin to see a movie and you quickly realize that the images projected against the wall are scenes from your life. You are watching a movie of some wonderful things you have managed to do and achieve. It can be really strange to see an image that had slipped from your mind. And as you watch you can recall the event and the memories can come flooding back. And you know from past experience that you can feel what you think, and now you feel changing sensations in your body as you relive that wonderful memory. As time moves on you may feel as if a burden were being taken from you. You have been transformed by the power of your mind, your emotions and your imagination.

And as you continued to enjoy the way you feel the movie changes pace and you find yourself looking at your hopes and dreams and wishes. You wonder how you can bring them to fruition. And then as if your thoughts were heard you remember the gift you picked up from the table below. You take it from your pocket and cup it gently in your hands. They may begin to tingle. And then you can close your eyes and breathe and focus and you hear yourself asking 'How can I best achieve my dreams?' And as you open your eyes you have a growing sense that you can have something special happen in your life. And you may not know what that something special may be but you do know that if you expect, it can happen. It can happen in its own special way in its own time and you know it will be perfect for you.

And as you think about your dream your thoughts appear projected on the wall in front of you. And as you see your thoughts in action you can have the feeling that you can achieve something you have always wanted. As you continue to watch, any weight of self-doubt that you have had can now lift from your shoulders as your feelings of confidence and certainty continue to grow. And you can take as much time as you need to gain the full benefit from this room. If you wish you can now become a part of the movie you have been watching. Find yourself stepping into your own body on the screen and notice how much more powerful and confident and certain you feel now. Play out the scene in the next few minutes and then find yourself naturally back in your comfy seat surrounded by a soft pink light. (*allow up to 5 minutes of uninterrupted visualization*)

As you find yourself in you seat you realize that it is time for you to leave this place now. You can walk down the stairway or take any other route you like back into the main cavern. You can take a last look at this special place before starting on the journey home. And as you walk you realize that this place is yours to visit whenever you feel like it. Whenever you need to make the time to listen to your inner self or to take a break from the bustle and demands of your outer world you now have a sanctuary. It is a place of peace and contentment where you can recharge your batteries, gather inspiration, let go of your problems and find appropriate wisdom.

As you make your way back across the landscape, breathing in the beauty and simplicity of this space, you may notice tiny changes in the environment. And you know that nature alters all the time. And even as it changes, whatever the season, you will always be able to find your way back.

Now once again become aware of your feet as they walk you back to the place where you began your journey. Soon, you will find your attention focused on the pages in this book and as you do so, you can become more and more aware of your feet on the floor.

Focus on your feet. Now feel the floor beneath you, flex your ankles and wiggle your toes. Stretch your body. Breathe in deeply and blow out hard. And again breathe in deeply and blow out hard. *Be ready to open your eyes.* Well done. Look around you. What colours can you see? Be aware of the ground beneath your feet before you stand up. OK, up you get. Now take a break in the fresh air and do something physical like gardening or playing with the kids.

Now just to reassure you that you are doing fine this is what other people have 'seen' whilst doing this exercise.

Harriet

'My sanctuary was a country rose garden, but the cavern was like an Arabian palace made of marble domes and pillars. The interior was decorated in burgundy and gold, very sparse, but very spacious and everything was made of the grey marble. My gift was a blue crystal cluster which glowed as I picked it up. Up the staircase was an attic room with bare floorboards and a sloping ceiling. A window looked out on a lush green landscape, very unlike the garden I had previously walked through. As I sat down in a scruffy old armchair and let the pink light flood over me, I didn't see any images of the past or the future – I drifted off into a kind of dream space, but it felt great, like I was suspended in the light, and very peaceful.'

Thea

'I was really surprised to find that almost as soon as I began to read the passage I found myself walking barefoot on sandy dusty ground. I was in a desert and it was cool. The atmosphere was incredibly peaceful. All I could hear was the wind and the sound of an eagle which flew ahead of me as if it were my guide. As the sun rose sidewinders surfed the dunes leaving swirling patterns in the sand. My sanctuary was in an oasis. The building was hidden by tall palm trees. I walked down into a gully to find the waterfall. I drank some water, it was sweet. I entered the sanctuary through a cave behind the waterfall. There were charcoal images etched into the stone walls. My gift was a radiant amethyst egg. My hand tingled as I held it. I climbed a stairway hewn from the rocks. It was round and cool under my feet. At the top I saw a huge cane and wood armchair, the cushions were feather-filled and made of red and orange silks. I sank into its comfort and watched my movies as if in a trance. I felt waves of energy moving through my body as the images changed. Afterward I felt elated. I am looking forward to going back.'

The great thing about this kind of sanctuary is that you don't have to go anywhere to reach it. All you need to do is close your eyes and, hey presto, you are there – if you are really troubled you will find the experience more valuable if you remember to shower under your waterfall first. Somehow this symbolically washes away any tension and leaves you more open to receive the gift of sanctuary 'time out'.

The more you practise the better able you will be at focusing on a productive and effective lifestyle and the less inclined you will be to let your imagination run away with you in a negative direction. Just as with the breathing exercises in Chapter 11, as you become more adept and conditioned to this technique, you will be able to use it to de-stress, affirm your commitment to a goal, improve your memory, prompt your unconscious to answer a question, or just to maintain your composure.

> *A man is not idle because he is absorbed in thought.*
> *There is visible labour, and there is invisible labour.*
> Victor Hugo 1862

20 Questions

Storytime

A muffled sound filtered into my dreams. The summons 'Mummy, mummy' broadcast from the dimly-lit nursery and swept through the darkened house. 'Mummy!' I emerged from my polycotton cocoon. 'Mummy! Mummy!' The shrill voice was urgent now. For the third time that night I shook my head and blinked as I lurched my tired body across the landing to Daniel's room 'Mu . . .' His cry was stifled as I lifted the duvet and joined him under the covers. I held Daniel close and swept my fingers through his hair. 'Well little one, what's the problem?' 'Mummy,' he said tearfully, 'there are monsters under the bed.' Set on getting some sleep I mumbled, 'I wonder what they are doing there?' as I carried Daniel into my room. 'We'll talk to them in the morning,' I said.

We woke to a blush-pink light. The sunrise was magnificent. Uneven swathes of colour dominated the skyline. It was a beautiful morning. 'Look, Daniel, heaven is pink today,' I said with a sense of wonder in my voice. Daniel observed the phenomenon for a while. 'Why do the shapes keep changing?' he asked. Without thinking, I said, 'That's the wind playing with the clouds.' Daniel frowned curiously. 'Are they having fun, do you think?' 'What do you think?' I asked, smiling. 'Maybe the clouds don't want to be played with right now.' I blinked in surprise. 'I never thought of that.' 'Wind is like monsters!' 'What did you say?' 'Wind is like monsters.' Daniel clenched his fists and bit his bottom lip. 'They push you around and wake you up and don't listen when you tell them to go away.' I was aghast. 'Monsters are like the wind? Does that mean they are invisible like the wind too?' 'Don't be silly.' 'Well, I never see them.' Daniel took me by the hand. 'They are shy.' 'How do you know that?' 'Well,' said Daniel thoughtfully, 'when you come to me they hide.' He led me to his room. Silently he pointed at the cavernous space beneath his bed. Whispering, I asked, 'Shall I take a look?' Daniel's eyes grew saucer-shaped as his eyebrows raised in anticipation of my next move. 'You might frighten them away?' Daniel said quizzically. I crouched on the floor and stretched my arm into the dark void. I waved it back and forth in a sweeping gesture. 'There is nothing here except for this.' I produced a long-lost toy. Unimpressed, Daniel shook his head. 'Oh Mummy, you scared them away.' 'How do you know?' 'I can feel them,' he said, 'let me look.' Daniel laid cheek down on the carpet. 'Do you think I can get them?' he said determinedly. 'But I thought you were afraid of monsters?' I was by now confused. If this was an exercise in reassurance it had worked beyond my expectation. 'Oh no,' he said, wriggling into the space under the bed, 'not when it's light, when it's light monsters are afraid of me!' I watched bemused as his feet disappeared. A few seconds later I heard mumbling followed by a stifled sneeze. My little boy slid feet first from the dusty space. 'They are very shy,' he sniffed, 'maybe that's why they only come out at night?' 'Ahh,' I said and nodded wisely leaving well alone.

Later we walked in the park. As always we stopped by the lake. We tossed bits of stale cake and broken biscuits to the wildfowl on the water. They were quite tame. Soon Daniel's boots were hidden in a flurry of feathers as milling birds pecked at the crumbs that fell at his feet. 'Mummy, how can I make friends with a shy monster?' The question took me by surprise. I looked at Daniel's feathered friends. 'Do you think monsters like cake?' Daniel licked his lips and popped a crumb in his mouth. 'Would you like to invite them to tea?' Daniel jumped at the thought and sent the birds flying. The moment we arrived home he ran to his room and dived under his bed. A few minutes later he strutted into the kitchen and triumphantly asked, 'Can I lay the table? They will be here soon!'

You can see that a question holds within it a world of possibility. If you are a newcomer to this idea then you may simply see a question as just another thought that passes through your mind. Questions do readily come to mind. What do you do to get yourself out of bed in the morning? Most people I know automatically start the day with an internal dialogue that runs something like – What's the time? What's the time? What day is it? Do I need to get up now? Have I got time for a lie-in? What shall I wear? Do I have time for breakfast? And, like Old Man River, that internal chatter just keeps rolling along. A question is rather like a Swiss army knife, one tool with many uses. Whatever you ask and however you ask, a question works something like this, it:

- Targets – pinpoints an objective
- Galvanizes – is a prompt
- Commands – is an instruction
- Observes – calls your mind to attention
- Stimulates – increases your curiosity and your awareness
- Instructs – is a call to action
- Inspires – excites and flexes your imagination
- Provokes – stretches the boundaries of your beliefs
- Investigates – allows you options and encourages experimentation
- Concentrates – requires focus
- Surveys – encourages study and inspection
- Analysis – seeks solutions
- Concludes – gets a result
- Educates – improves your communication

When used to its best advantage it is a powerful commodity. How can you make the best use of this remarkable tool? The answer is to sharpen up your questioning (and thinking) ability. This is necessary because we often use language lazily. For instance, a kitchen knife can be used to replace a screwdriver and a frying pan can be a substitute for a wok – but they will do the job in the best and most efficient way? Generally speaking people have a tendency toward lax thinking. This does not mean that we are all lazy. We learn to talk, and thereby to think, by emulating our parents and peers. They learnt from their parents and peers. In English a 🐄 is a *cow* because we have labelled it that way. A 🐄 is not termed a *cow* when speaking French or German. A 🐄 becomes named a *cow* by accident and for convenience's sake it stays that way. This is true of all language.

Taking this into consideration, it is likely that you will frequently express phrases and ideas that are thoroughly entrenched within your speech. They will be patterns that you repeat. They are often routine and you will say them without thinking and think them without noticing. Has anyone ever told you that 'you sound just like your father'? Have you heard yourself repeating a phrase you heard on the TV? Don't we all know the sayings 'money doesn't grow on trees' or 'big boys don't cry' or 'rules are there to be broken'? Whether we realize it or not every time we articulate in this way we re-condition ourselves to use them again and again. Some, like 'please', 'thank you', 'I love you' and 'stop it now!' are really useful. Others, like the kitchen knife mentioned earlier, may not be the best tool for the job.

A lazy question is one that leads your mind – and your life for that matter – into a loop. In ever-decreasing spirals like a black hole, they draw on your attention and absorb your mind. By then (horror of horrors) the light of inspiration has been obscured and you can find yourself at the bottom of a shaft with no obvious way out – until you ask a 'quality question', that is!

Lazy thinking and subsequently lazy questions can be generated from self-depreciating and self-defeatist statements like:

'Why am I so useless?'
'She's so slim, why can't I look like that?'
'Nothing I do is ever good enough, is it?'
'Why can't I do better?'

Now if you ask questions like that what kind of answers do you think you might hear?

Q: 'Why am I so useless?'

A: 'Because you're lazy. You never do anything right. Why can't you be like Joanna Blog-Perfect? She wouldn't be in this ridiculous mess.'

Q: 'Why can't I do better?'

A: 'You never were very good at this kind of thing. Do you remember that time in school when you failed the maths test? I don't know why you even bother. You know you will only show yourself up. Why would you even want to try when other people are so much better at it than you? I'd give up now and save yourself some embarrassment.'

I'm certain that the examples above will have rung a few bells, generated some discomfort and called you to attention. Without realizing it you can exacerbate a problem or build a mountain from a molehill simply by talking to yourself in this way. So what can you do about it? How can you remodel this habit and turn it into something constructive?

You can generate good 'quality questions'. These act like booster rockets. They help you to turn things around and give you the momentum needed to extricate yourself from that downward spiral I talked about earlier. Liberated, your mind is free to traverse a universe of limitless space and infinite possibility.

A question is the tool of masterminds

To make the best use of a question you will need to *un-learn* many of your current question-behaviour and attitudes. Simultaneously you can *re-educate* yourself in question expertise and etiquette. Re-training takes some effort. You may need to exercise some self-discipline – incidentally asking yourself appropriate questions is highly motivating and will help to keep you on track! Your results will be rapid and more than worth the time you have invested. One of my students quoted.

> *'Learning about questions has opened my mind to a new realm of possibilities. I have been compelled to recognize that I have choices. My self-confidence has increased and I now feel as if I have control of my destiny.'*

Before you move on to some practical exercises I would like to divert your attention for a moment. Let us set a scene. Think of yourself as a conductor. You have the privilege of leading a chorus of internal voices. Now they babble and whisper at will. To prepare for your debut performance you will need to guide and arrange these chattering voices. Compose yourself. Your baton is a tool. It has the qualities of a question. Now as you tap it on your podium, all those voices come momentarily to attention. Expectantly they await your next instruction. Each is focused on the movement of a hand or nod of your head. You begin to direct, and as you maintain composure the voices synthesize and flow. Your choir follows your lead precisely. It does exactly what you ask of it. As you relax and focus on the direction of your thoughts your vision is actualized. You are orchestrating a symphony of harmonious thought? How does it sound? How does it feel? What does it look like? Could it be even better? How will you find out? You may think about it.

You can make the transition from chattering voices to mental symphony by exploring and experimenting with the guidelines below.

Many questions begin with a stem. By this I mean:

- How . . . ?
- What . . . ?
- Where . . . ?
- Who . . . ?
- Why . . . ?

Lazy questions often start with either a why . . . ? or a what if . . . ?

- Why can't I look like that?
- What if I can't find another job?
- Why did he get promoted?
- What if I'm not good enough?
- Why can't things be different?
- What if I'm made redundant?
- Why did this happen to me?

- What if she's having an affair?
- Why doesn't he love me?

This type of thinking encourages intellectualization and often results in speculation, making something up, and presumption. Wondering what others are thinking or doing, for that matter, is a complete waste of time. Think about this for a moment. You can never know precisely what is going on in someone else's head. Come to think about it, they probably don't know what's going on in there half the time either! Refocus your energy. Take the time you spend worrying and reinvest it in yourself. Master your imagination by thinking happy thoughts and while you're feeling good take time to learn how to ask quality questions. Your imagination is your best friend and you know how to use it. You can focus your mind in any direction you like. If you need information ask a question. Gather together some good quality reliable data and use it well. The exercises below will help you to restructure the way you use questions so they can be to your best advantage.

To develop quality questions simply change the stem by experimenting with the ones below.

- How . . . ? How can . . . ? How can I . . . ?
- What can I do to . . . ? What needs to happen to . . . ?
- Where can . . . ? Where can I . . . ? Where can I find . . . ?
- When can . . . ? When can I . . . ? When can I have . . . ?

Thus the question 'Why can't I look like that?' becomes:

- How can I look like that?
- What can I do to look like that?
- When can I look like that?

And the question 'What if I can't find another job?' becomes:

- How can I find another job?
- What can I do to find another job?
- Where can I find another job?
- When can I have another job?

See the difference? Feel the difference? Now it's your turn.

Exercise 🖎

Use the remaining example questions above and practise changing the stems. Obviously, if you follow my words to the letter some of the sentences you create will not make sense. Just cross them out and use the ones that work well for you.

Now to every rule there is an exception – especially when we talk about language. Can you guess what would happen if you applied those rules to a question like 'Why am I so useless?' It would look something like this!

- How am I so useless?
- What can I do (to be) so useless?
- Where can I (be) so useless?
- When can I (be) so useless?

Following the rules in this instance only confirm the self-defeating belief that you can be useless. This is counterproductive. Therefore in this case to develop a 'quality question' and get a positive result you will need to be a little more creative.

Exercise 🖎

Whenever you notice that you have used a self-defeating word to describe yourself, find at least three complementary or positive words to take its place like so:

- Lazy – Active/Motivated/Eager
- Fat – Robust/Fit/Healthy
- Useless – Useful/Helpful/Effective
- Stupid – Resourceful/Discerning/Inventive

Now substitute the self-defeating word with the complementary word. 'Why am I so useless?' becomes:

- How can I be useful?
- What can I do (to be) helpful?
- Where can I be effective?

Can you see the difference? How does it feel? What can you tell me about it? OK, now that you've got the idea it's your turn. Use the remaining example questions as before and practice changing the stems and substituting words. Be creative and discerning. Keep a note of the questions that work best for you.

> *Learning is not attained by chance.*
> *It must be sought for with ardour*
> *and attended to with diligence.*
>   Abigaile Adams 1780

Another problem that many people seem to experience is a reluctance to ask, either for information or for what they need. They have a mistaken idea that they will be thought of as stupid, uninformed, demanding, or even self-indulgent. Often people will not quench their curiosity or allay their concerns for fear of embarrassment or rejection.

Now we could spend the next few paragraphs discussing where this problem came from but it wouldn't necessarily make a difference to your life – other than making you feel even worse that is. Furthermore, every time you run through the problem in your mind's eye, listen to your internal script and feel those uncomfortable feelings. You can simply convince yourself that whatever it is, it is insurmountable – here comes that ever-decreasing spiral again. Stop! Hold it. Be still. How you are going to get out of this now? What's the best thing that can happen? How soon will that happen? What will be the most productive result?

It makes sense to think that we can get what we want by asking for what we need. However, it seems that some people believe they can have their needs met by telling you what they want to avoid.

- 'What do you want for dinner?' 'I don't want pizza.'
- 'Can we get some exercise?' 'I don't like running.'
- 'Well, what do you want from this relationship?' 'I don't want to talk about it!'

Really, the best way to have something is to be direct about it. Ask for enchiladas if that is your taste. If you prefer shooting hoops to running, say so. If you want more love express it affectionately. You have a right to ask for anything you want. Others have the right to comply and the right to refuse. There is a saying 'If at first you don't succeed try, try, try again.' This does not mean putting on the pressure, demanding, nagging or sulking. It means asking around. Someone somewhere will have what you need and will be willing to let you have it. Be intelligent. If you need a loan it's no good asking a friend who is broke to lend you money. Even if they wanted to help they could not. If you need that cash in a hurry you may have to go to a bank, or do some extra work. Know what I mean? Good.

When you focus on an outcome the problem will take care of itself

Now let's be upfront and honest. Regardless of good intentions and even with all the best self-help and will-power in the world anyone can have a challenging day. Chattering monkeys are mischievous creatures. They delight in finding fresh and innovative ways to test your newly acquired skills. (You can go back to Chapters 12 and 13 to practise breaking the habit of chattering thinking.) Whatever happens, no matter how irritated or disconcerted you may find yourself at any moment, you can remember that there is possibility in everything. So, each time you come across a lazy thought or unconstructive question you can take a moment and change it into something of quality. Practice not only makes perfect it also makes a new habit.

The best way to break a habit is to create a new one

Part 3

21 The land that time forgot

During Parts 1 and 2 of this book you have been introduced to the idea that your mind is like a vast inner landscape. I call this the *metascape* due to its dreamlike and metaphorical nature. The word *metaphor* has many definitions. For the purposes of this section of the programme, we are going to take metaphor to mean a *representation*.

In Chapter 17, you saw how picturesque our speech can be. You also know that speech is a verbalized thought and as you think you can see an image and you may also experience a feeling. In this section of the book you will be exploring the idea that the way we speak accurately represents your metascape (inner landscape), and that your metascape actually influences how you speak (by now you will have begun to explore your metascape and therefore discovered for yourself its richness and diversity).

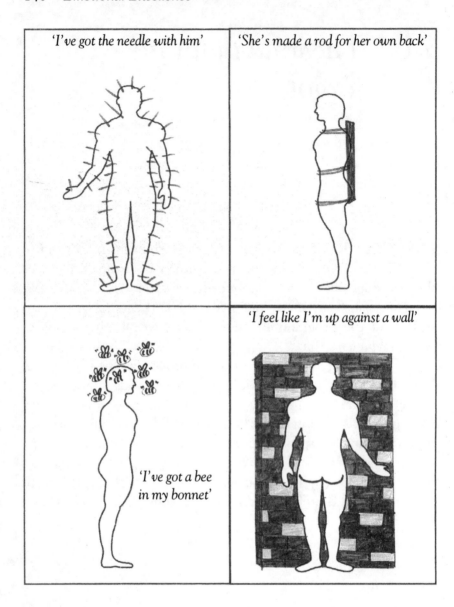

Without wanting to seem too repetitive I am going to once again refer to Chapter 17 in order to remind you that your unconscious mind uses metaphor when it wants to:

- Make sense of something it doesn't yet understand
- Observe and remember information

- Memorize events and experiences
- Communicate and express itself

Whether you realize it or not, you will automatically form a metaphor from each and every experience you have ever had. Metaphors will develop from real-life events, from your imagination, or as a combination of the two. It is a natural function that helps you to store the complexity of your experience in a simple way, in the same way that a picture is broken down and digitally stored as dots of information on a CD-ROM. When you need access to this information your brain reconstitutes the memory and represents it to you as an image, a thought, a physical sensation and in some rare cases even as a taste or smell:

- 'I was so nervous my head was swimming and I felt sick to the stomach.'
- 'The sound of church bells ringing takes me back to Sunday mornings as a child.'
- 'Every time I think of falling in love my heart leaps and I see fireworks.'
- 'I didn't trust him, something smelt fishy to me.'

As we use metaphor *in* language, within your metascape metaphor *is* a language. It is non-verbal in nature, non-literal and coded. It can also be abstract. It is a teller of stories. It is often evocative and motivating and can rekindle emotion and memories. When visual it can be disparate and dreamlike, appearing as a kaleidoscope of apparently disjointed images. When physical it can appear as odd aches, pains and sensations. These can include the source of unresolved chronic illnesses. Metaphor acts as a messenger from your unconscious and in spite of the difference in language and structure your conscious mind is expected to understand it!

In order to make sense of these messages, it is important to grasp that metaphor is simply *information*. It is not exact. Metaphor is a comparison and an interpretation that is stored in shorthand. To your conscious mind it cannot be taken as literal. What you see is definitely not what you get!

Learning how to decipher and communicate within your metascape is not a subject that you can approach with logic in mind. Rather like a Klingon in *Startrek*, if you attempt to make sense of it in a conventional way you might, to say the least, run the risk of becoming confused and frustrated. So, if this is the case, why are we bothering with it at all?

To answer the question, think of the saying 'you are what you think' and 'you are what you feel'. Everything that you think and feel is represented by metaphor within your metascape. Therefore, metaphor is a unique and wonderful resource. Contained within the images, sensations, sounds, tastes and smells that make up its nature is information about you.

Through metaphor you can access codes that are the blueprints of the deep structure of your beliefs, behaviour and identity. These access codes run your personality and performance programmes. When you know how the programmes run you can use them to their best advantage. Furthermore, should you wish to achieve rapid and permanent changes in any area of your life all you need to do is modify the code. The result is a natural, non-threatening, self-generated, automatic sequence of transformation.

In order to get the greatest benefit from your natural ability to form metaphors I am going to introduce you to Emotional Mapping. This is a technique that I have developed over the past five years during workshops and one-to-one sessions. In preparation for the next phase of this course we look at how and where you store your metaphors and memories.

Think of a lemon. What does it look like? How does it smell? If you cut it open and squeeze a drop of juice on your tongue, what happens? Take a few moments to allow your responses to develop.

How quickly did you notice you were salivating?

Isn't it interesting how just thinking of a lemon can create a digestive response. The thought was a trigger. By the same token, had you tasted lemon juice whilst blindfolded, you would have 'seen' a lemon.

You don't know consciously how these connections are made, but you make them anyway. This is because somewhere in your bodymind, somewhere within your metascape there is a record or file full of 'information on lemons'.

Have you ever noticed anyone daydreaming? They seem to be staring into space. Sometimes they can look straight through you; they may not be seeing you at all. Their eyes are fixed in space while their mind plays a movie in another time-frame. How can it be that your vision can ignore something physically 'here' in preference for something 'over there'? That 'something over there' is in your metascape.

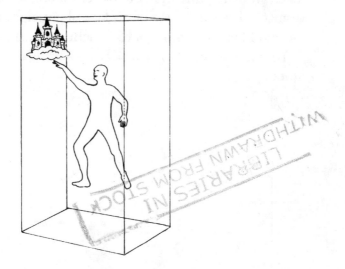

Think of your metascape as an area that exists *outside* your body.

You can remember a time when you have been extremely excited or frightened. You have heard of the saying 'I've got butterflies in my tummy'. What about repulsion or disgust? – 'It makes my skin crawl.'

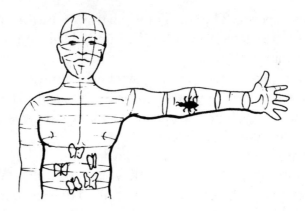

Think of your metascape as an area that exists *inside* your body.

At times you will experience your metascape from many different places at once. For instance, when thinking of my son I feel a glowing pride in my upper chest and a warm feeling in my stomach. I see an image of his face about eight inches in front of me and I hear a memory of his laughter across the room.

Your metascape can be as **BIG** as a universe, or smaller than an atom.

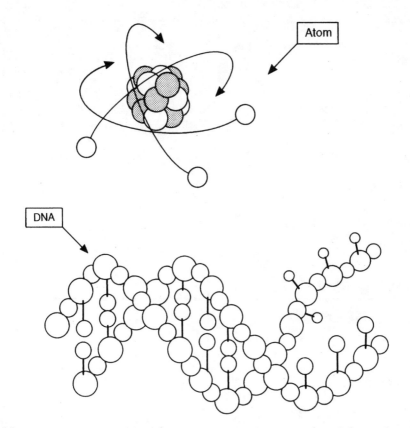

Here is an opportunity for you to experience what I have been talking about:

First, do your stretch and relax exercises.
Then answer the following questions and record the details in your workbook:

- Where is happy?
- How do you know that's happy?
- How does it look?
- How does it sound?
- How does it feel?

Now you have investigated 'happy', what's a happy when it's happy like that? Here's an example:

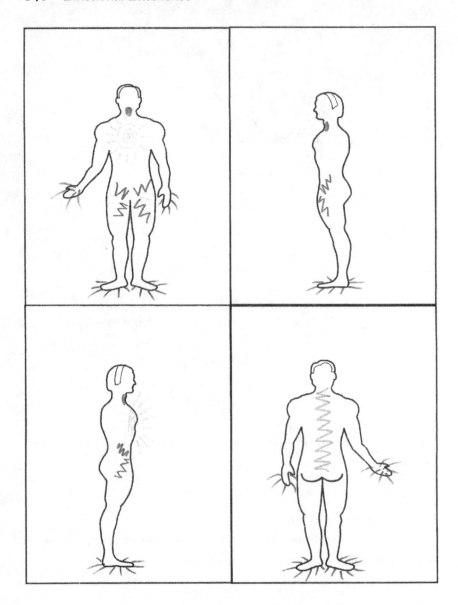

This person feels 'happy' within their body

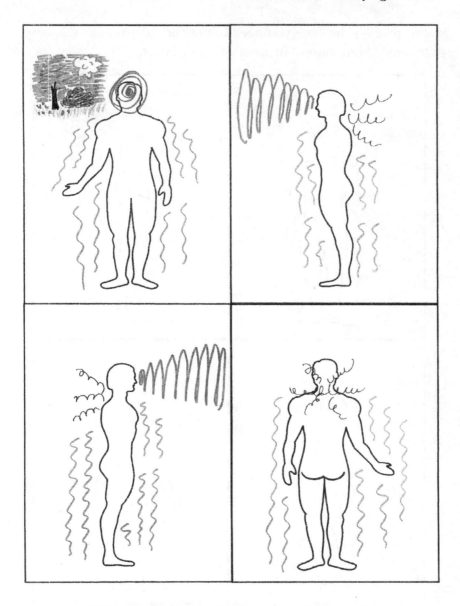

This person feels or notices 'happy' outside their body

Now take all the time you need to put the information you have gathered about 'happy' on your 3D body chart

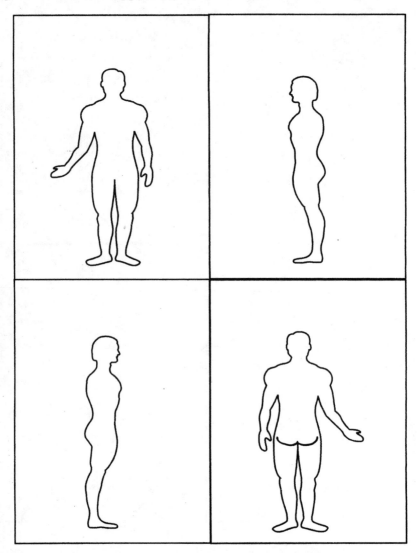

OK, now that you have explored 'happy' let's look at 'sad'. When you feel sad how do you experience it? Record the results in your workbook.

- Where is sad?
- How do you know that's sad?

- How does it look?
- How does it sound?
- How does it feel?

Now you have investigated 'sad', what's a sad when it's sad like that?
Here's an example:

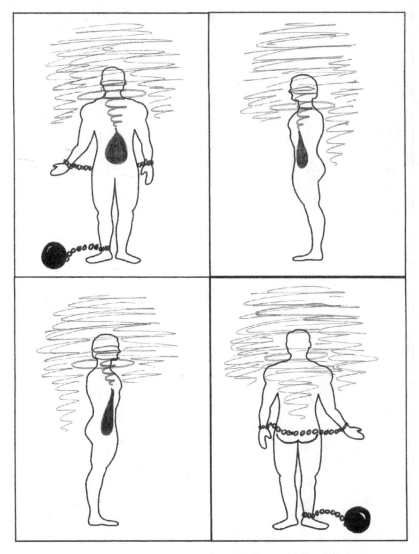

*Note: This person experiences 'sad' inside and outside the body
simultaneously*

Using the information on 'sad' that you gathered earlier do yours now.

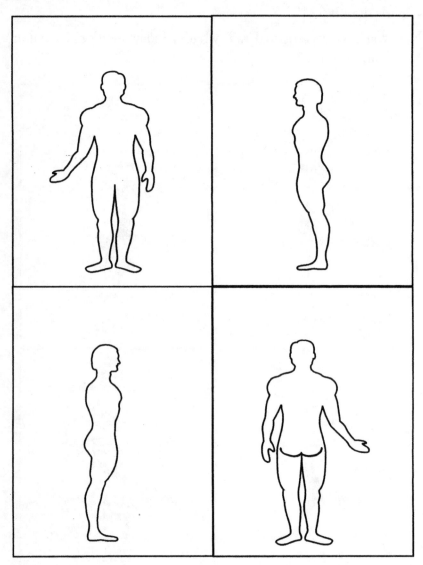

Well done. You have just completed this lesson. Now choose some feelings you would like to explore using the methods described in this chapter and go for it!

The physical body gives the truest image of the human spirit

22 Emotional mapping for beginners

Jordie: 'What's happening?'
Data: 'I am uncertain. Because I am unfamiliar with emotion I am unable to articulate the sensation.'
                                        Star Trek, The Next Generation

Emotional Mapping is a way of recording and deciphering information from your metascape. Initially it may look a little like Tony Buzan's Mind Maps. However, any resemblance is purely incidental – which is probably to be expected as connections exist between the ideas and will not detract from the value of either. Unlike other methods of mapping, Emotional Maps work with information from your metascape. The information you are about to gather and record is about you. It will be as distinctive and unique to you as your fingerprints.

The method is designed as a practical exercise in self-awareness and self-recognition. As you become familiar with the process you will find yourself gaining powerful insights about deep-seated behaviour patterns and intuitive flashes that help to resolve what had previously seemed to be insurmountable problems.

You will begin by following and answering specific questions that elicit information about how you keep your issue or problem behaviour in place. By recording your responses in the way of a map, you will be able to keep track of your actions and reactions. Many of these will be automatic or beyond conscious awareness and you only become aware of them because the question has prompted you to focus your attention in that direction. The result of your efforts will be a visual representation in words and images. You then have the chance to have cognitive knowledge of your behaviour. Knowledge is power. Armed with this information you can choose to make a difference in your life.

In the same way, you can utilize the Emotional Mapping technique to develop solutions. You can ask yourself questions about how you have made successful changes and transitions in the past. Your mapped answers will indicate the strategies that you need to employ and apply to the area in question in order to initiate significant and lasting change.

All the exercises that you have done up to this point will ensure that you can learn this technique easily and quickly. Before we go any further you are going to need some basic equipment.

This will include:

- Plenty of plain paper. A3 sized is best
- A surface on which you can spread yourself out
- Sticky tape
- Coloured pens and crayons
- Something to write with
- A comfy chair – make sure you can place both feet flat on the floor

Or

- A favourite piece of floor – with a wall on which to rest your back
- Cushions, a rug or blanket
- Some uninterrupted time – set your answerphone and switch off the phone please

I am going to take you through this step by step. These exercises and instructions have been road tested on many occasions. They work. If you do find yourself getting confused take a break, backtrack and start from the beginning.

The first lesson begins here. Below is a training map. It works a little like those dot to dot puzzles you played as a child.

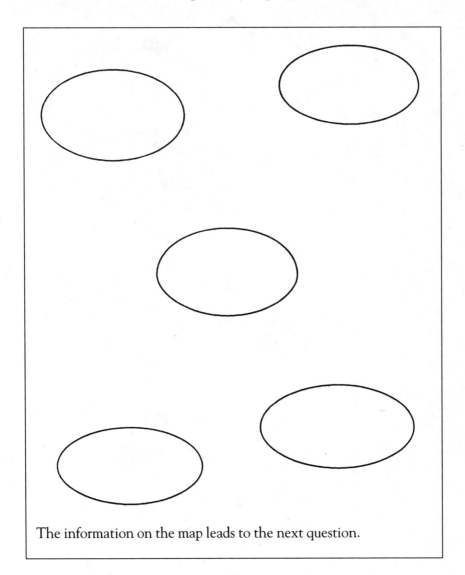

The information on the map leads to the next question.

And this is what it should look like when it's finished:

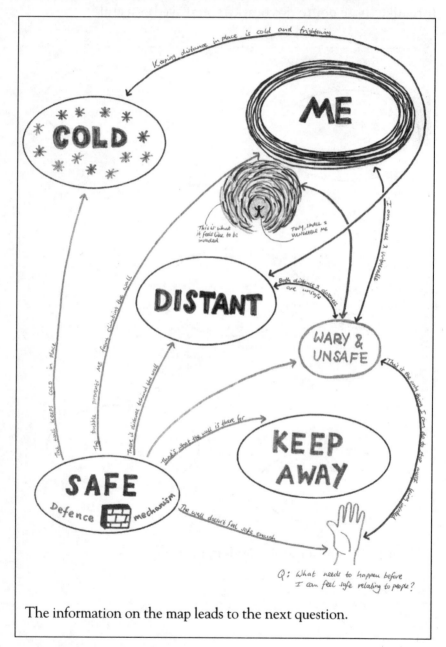

The information on the map leads to the next question.

The following training map was constructed by Harriet by following a series of specific instructions. It is a great example of how Emotional Mapping can be a reminder of what is already known intellectually. In picture form Harriet's emotional recognition was much more immediate. The impact was greater and it brought home to her the realization that SHE had created the problem, albeit unwittingly. Harriet soon recognized that she was responsible for her outcomes and therefore also had the power to make whatever changes she needed in order to resolve it. As you read through Harriet's art work please follow the instructions methodically as you will be duplicating them later.

Harriet's Training Map

1. Do the relaxation exercise in Chapter 1.

2. In order to find Harriet's issue she asked herself: *'What would I like to have different in my life?'*

3. Her answer was: *'I would like a loving committed relationship.'* Is this a specific question or a specific statement? If you begin mapping on a specific statement, the first question is always: 'What's it like not to have/be it?' Harriet's statement is: 'I would like a committed loving relationship.'

4. Harriet asked herself *'What's it like not to have it?'* Her immediate reaction was a feeling of overall coldness. She said 'Cold', and then wrote COLD on the training map and drew snowflakes around it, like so:

The information on the map leads to the next question.

5. Harriet asked herself, 'What does ✱COLD✱ mean to me?' Her immediate response was an image of a blue bubble around her which keeps her distant. She drew this on her map, like so:

The information on the map leads to the next question.

6. Looking at the map, Harriet asked herself '*And what does* DISTANT *mean to me?*' Her immediate response was to put out her arm and say, 'Keep away'. She drew this on her map, like so:

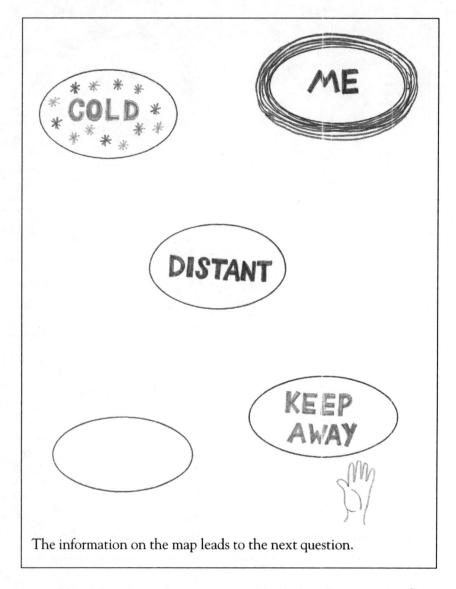

The information on the map leads to the next question.

7. Looking at the map, Harriet asked herself: '*What is it like to* ✋ *?*' She said: 'Safe!' vehemently and felt adamant. She said, ' "Safe" looked like a wall.' She drew this on the map, like so:

The information on the map leads to the next question.

Harriet had filled in all her bubbles. There is a lot of information here to work with. As well as the words, we also have images of a hand , a wall  and a blue bubble .

8. Now is the time to review your art work. Look at it for a few moments and then ask '*What attracts you the most?*' Harriet's immediate response was, 'The wall .' We now focus our attention on the wall and use it as the central point on the map by asking '*What's the connection between*  *. . . ?*' and

every other image or word on the map, drawing an arrow to connect them like so . . .

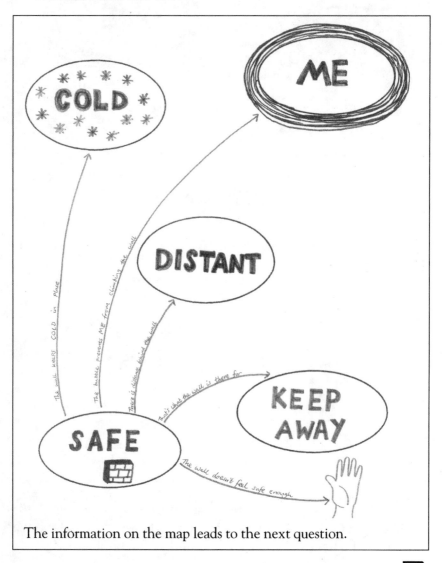

The information on the map leads to the next question.

9. Harriet asked herself, '*What's the connection between this* and ⟨*COLD*⟩?' Harriet closed her eyes, stared into space and after a few seconds said: 'The wall is what keeps it cold.' She then drew an arrow and wrote 'Wall keeps ⟨*COLD*⟩ in place' along the length of the arrow.

10. Harriet asked herself, '*What is the connection between* 🧱 *and* (ME) *?*' Harriet closed her eyes. After a few moments she laughed and drew an arrow between 🧱 and (ME) and wrote 'The bubble prevents me from climbing the wall.'

11. Harriet asked herself, '*What is the connection between* 🧱 *and* (DISTANT)*?*' She closed her eyes, screwed up her face and then drew an arrow between 🧱 and (DISTANT). She wrote 'There is distance behind the wall.'

12. Harriet asked herself, '*What's the connection between* 🧱 *and* (KEEP AWAY) *?*' Harriet closed her eyes, her lips puckered. She drew an arrow and wrote 'That's what the wall is there for.'

13. Harriet asked herself, '*What is the connection between* 🧱 *and* 🖐 *?*' She closed her eyes and bit her bottom lip. She drew an arrow and wrote 'The wall doesn't feel safe enough.'

Harriet has gathered a huge amount of information about what it is like not to have a loving committed relationship in her life. The map also indicates that she has some resistance to getting close to people. Much of the information is encoded in visual metaphor: 🧱, 🖐, (ME), 'There is distance behind the wall' etc . . . and some is encoded in the body movements she made when asking herself questions.

14. With so much available information, it is important at this stage to *review* the Emotional Map. Harriet asked herself, 'What have I discovered so far?' After a few minutes of looking over her map Harriet said: 'What I have discovered so far is that I seem to have a lot of fear attached to relating. There is a great distance between me and most other people, although keeping the distance in place is cold and frightening in itself. The wall appears to represent my defence mechanism in keeping people away, although I still feel wary and unsafe even when the wall is there. The question that springs to mind from all this information is "*What do I need to do in order to resolve this issue?*" I'm really

surprised to have gathered this amount of information in under an hour.'

15. Having done a review the next step is to write or draw any extra information you have gathered. Harriet added 'defence mechanism' under her wall, and linked (*COLD*) and (DISTANT) with an arrow, writing along it. She added another bubble WARY & UNSAFE, and wrote her question in the bottom right-hand corner like so:

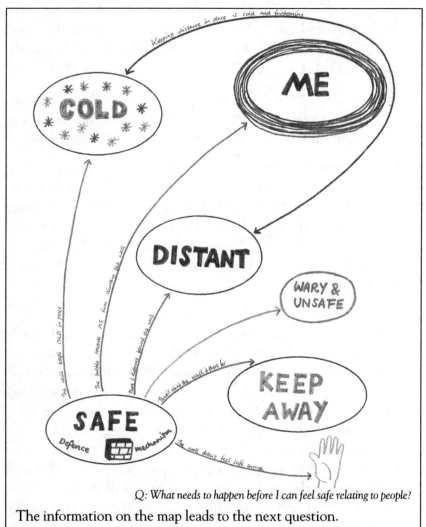

Q: What needs to happen before I can feel safe relating to people?

The information on the map leads to the next question.

Having completed her review, she then asked herself, '*What further connections can I make?*' She then wrote and drew her immediate responses on the map, like so:

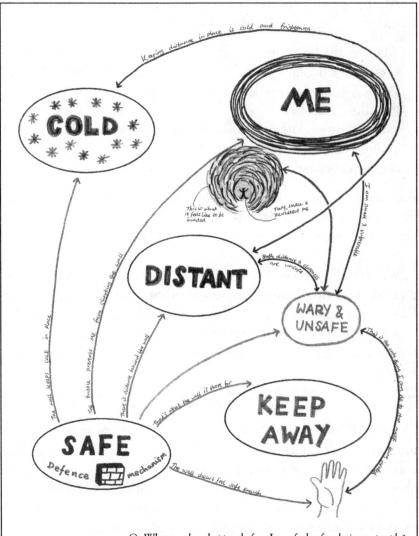

Q: What needs to happen before I can feel safe relating to people?

The information on the map leads to the next question.

Although we could go on asking more questions about this map, Harriet had now gathered sufficient information to give her tremendous insight into her behaviour around relationships. This information could now be used in finding a solution and making a permanent change.

At this point, Harriet felt it was appropriate to review her Emotional Map again. This is what she recognized:

> 'Making further connections between bubbles has given me even more insight into what makes me so scared of most relationships. Somewhere in my subconscious is the belief that if I allow people to get too close I will become invaded and swallowed up. This information can now be used as a basis to finding a solution for change, although already it explains a lot about my behaviour throughout my life.'

As you will have seen by following Harriet's training map, Emotional Mapping gives you a structure upon which you can track the process of your deep-rooted beliefs, emotional status and behavioural patterns.

Whatever you may discover during your mapping exercise the process does not require or benefit from analysis. You may be looking for reasons, excuses, justifications or judgements, but, as in Chapter 8, you will benefit best by simply taking the information you gather as read, seen, heard or felt, in other words:

It is what it is

On your Emotional Map you will develop an awareness of the mechanisms of your current issue. Once you know how it works, you can modify or redesign it any way you like. In the next chapters, you will be developing your Emotional Mapping skills and techniques in such a way as to make a beneficial and productive difference to your life. To do that effectively, you will need to follow the instructions on how to develop a training map. Please use the maps supplied to get the feel of Emotional Mapping.

You can practise using one of the statements or questions below. Remember, this is your first try. This method has been tried, tested, adjusted, retested and perfected!

The most common start-up problem we have seen comes from mappers *not following the instructions verbatim*. If you have gone through the troubleshooting section and you are still lost and confused, go back to the beginning of this chapter. Read through it again slowly and then have another go. If all else fails, you can E-Mail us on motex@geocities.com. We may be able to help you with your query.

Once you have successfully completed your training maps, draw some for yourself. You can stick to this format for as long as you like. For some of my students training maps have become too restrictive and they prefer to work with blank sheets of paper building up a series of words and images placed randomly. If you choose to work in this way remember that the method of connecting each word and image with arrows remains the same.

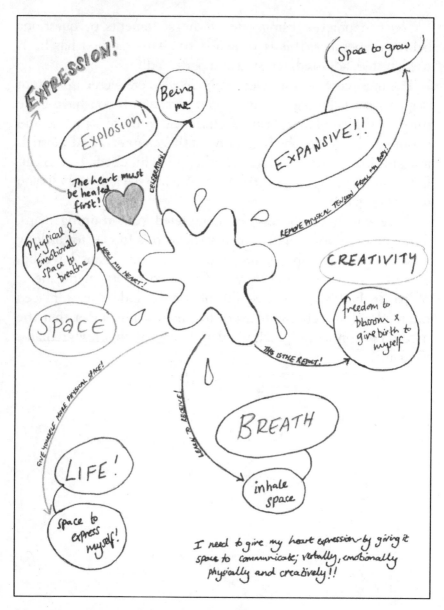

Here are some tips for really great maps:

- *Use large A3+ sized paper* (Stick smaller sheets together if you need to) or your Emotional Map will become cramped and it may be difficult to fit in and decipher all the information.

- *Make it colourful.* This adds interest, and the colours you choose can be informative too.
- *Put down every response you have* no matter how irrelevant, silly uncomfortable or embarrassing it may seem. Often it's the things we try to censor that tell us the most about the issue at hand.
- *Go back to the beginning of this chapter again,* read it over, do your relaxation exercise, then go for it!

Here are some issues you may like to explore:

- How would I behave if I wasn't afraid?
- How can I have or create more money?
- How can I become more healthy?
- What do I get out of my job?
- How would I do better at my studies?
- What happens when I get angry/upset/frightened/despondent?
- What are the benefits and pitfalls of my relationship?

An Emotional Map is a cross-section of your metascape. You have taken a slice, put it on a slide and looked at it under a microscope. To find out how and where this information is placed both in and around your body, take the words and images from your completed map and put them on a 3D bodychart, like so:

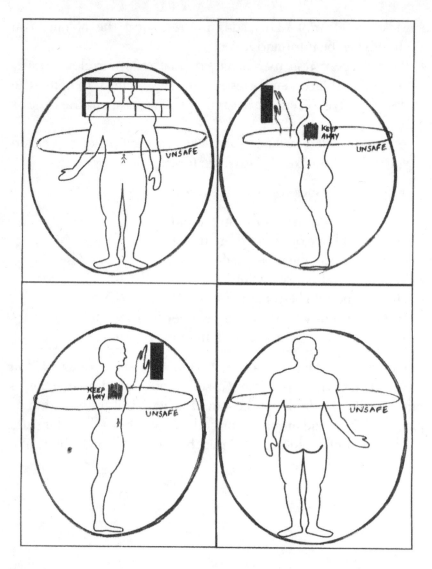

This can be helpful in preparing you for the next stage of Emotional Mapping:

Harriet: 'It grounds the information and makes it feel like it's part of me, rather than a lot of detached images and words on a page. It reminds me that the information has come from me. In order to be able to resolve this issue, I need to know that it's mine.'

Charlie: 'I find it easier to process information when I feel it is detached from me. Making it into images and placing it on a bodychart in this way helps me to deal with it better.'

Please use the 3D bodychart below to record the information from your map now.

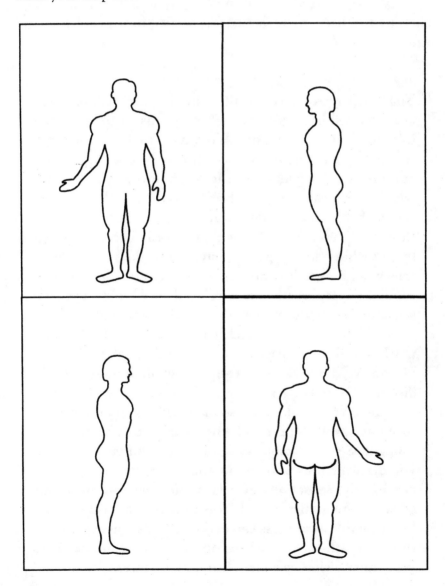

Well done. Now I would like you to realize that there is no mystery about the exercises you have just completed. You have simply learned a technique that has shown you how to become consciously aware of information about yourself that up until now has been beyond your conscious awareness.

Now take a short break. Get up, walk around, stretch and come back to the book to read the following Multi Level Reading exercise.

You have read exercises like this before, and on each occasion you have noticed that the words on the page can initiate a state of relaxation. You know that you can learn so much when you are relaxed. It may be that you can be curious to know what you can learn now as you wonder whether you can reach a relaxed state in exactly the same way as before, or whether you will discover a new route this time? You already know that you can become relaxed by breathing in a special way. How does your body remember how to breathe when you want to relax? As you recall how to breathe in a relaxed way, these growing sensations can develop with the rise and fall of your chest. How would you read if you read to a rhythm like that? How does the pace of your breathing link to the pace of your reading? So, you can read while quite naturally discovering relaxing pleasure. There are so many things that can give you pleasure, so many things you know how to enjoy. And your mind knows how to find a happy thought. So as it comes to mind, what can you notice as you discover how your mind and body work together to develop the sensations of relaxation, that can grow and grow as you notice them? You can be comfortable now knowing this awareness can evolve, and as you experience those sensations you can encounter that memory just as your inner vision becomes clearer and clearer.

Now, you know each memory has its own images and feelings and sensations. As you hold this book in your hands you can also grasp new concepts and ideas as easily as you can read these words. And you may be curious to discover how that is possible. You see, as you were reading you may have wondered many things, and as you have listened to the words with inner ears you can now bring to mind many other times when learning was so easy. There have been times when you had a sense of something and yet did not quite understand everything there is to know about it. And there are times when you realize that you have remembered something that you did not know that you knew. Good. Now, you can have so many experiences like this in your life. How will you notice you can do that? Wouldn't you say it may be interesting to find out? You can remember that once upon a time, you did not understand the meaning of writing. You did not know then that the shapes you now see are words. And when you did not understand letters and words, you may have looked for pictures. A picture represents a thousand words and a thousand words can paint a picture. You can get the picture now. Any picture is an image and you can imagine what it would be like to understand something that you really want to know. What do you sense as you make sense and gain clarity? How does a small child discover and learn by looking at a page? You will know because a distant memory like that can be so useful now. And you can enhance the best parts of a memory like that and just allow the rest to fade away as you read. You can be comfortable now knowing the best parts can evolve. So, how will you experience those sensations? They can just form at this time as your inner vision becomes clearer and clearer in exactly the right way. Now, you may notice how a changing image can develop changing sensations within your body. How is it that a mind and body can develop together to rediscover those sensations? What might those sensations be as you relax into the process and gain more understanding? What can you perceive about these links that will be even more useful as they grow and grow? And you can cultivate and encourage the best kind of feelings that you can. For as you feel better and better you may discover that you will be delightfully surprised by the result.

Now, in your own way become aware of your breathing. Remember how any natural breathing rhythm can relax your mind and body. And as you recall what it is like to breathe rhythmically you can retain your new discoveries as the images fade away. It can be pleasing to recognize how the rise and fall of your chest can extend these growing sensations of relaxation as your mind becomes more alert. How does it feel to be relaxed and alert at the same time? As you continue to read this passage you will soon realize the benefit of these words. So what might that benefit be? How will you continue to discover it as your mind comes to full alertness now. As you receive all the benefit you may take some time to sit quietly and integrate new realizations as your breath flows through your body. Soon it will be time for you to put this book down and stretch and do something completely different for a while. So, you can continue to remember to accelerate your learning and implement so many constructive outcomes.

Now breathe and focus on your feet. You can feel the floor beneath you. Now focus on your feet and as you feel them flex and wiggle your toes. Stretch your body. Breathe in deeply and blow out hard. And again breathe deeply in and blow out hard. *Now stretch your body and open your eyes.* Look around you. What colours can you see? Clap your hands several times. That was an illuminating experience. Well done. Now do something physical like washing the dishes, mowing the lawn or working out.

23   Gathering resources

Now that you are fully aware of the dynamics of your issue, it is time to seek out information that will lead to a solution, resolution or beneficial change in the situation. We call this gathering resources. This is like blackberry picking in autumn. You take a basket, with the intention to fill it with the cream of the crop. You then need to find a thorny blackberry bush. Once you have the fruit within reach you can carefully pick the juiciest, plumpest berries to take home. To make the best pie or jam you will need to leave behind the fruits that are past their best, and those that are still to ripen.

Resources can be gathered from:

- Any current successful behaviour or belief
- Any past successful behaviour or belief
- Experimenting with new behaviour or beliefs
- Learning a new skill
- Copying or emulating another's successful behaviour
- Intuitive flashes, images and other information from your unconscious – one client uses the attributes of characters from *Star Trek*
- Your metascape

Some resources are universal. This means that whenever they are applied to any kind of problem there will be some relief. A universal resource map may look something like this, or contain words and images of this nature:

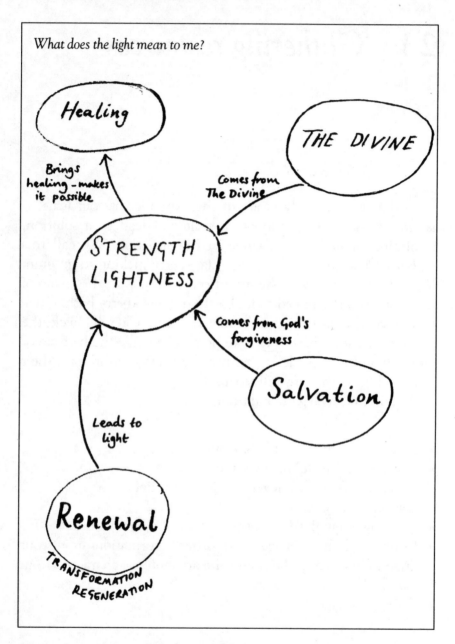

What does the light mean to me?

Amanda's map was very useful as a source of information. However, the fact that she used words indicated that she was dealing with this problem on an intellectual level. In order to add more depth to her experience I asked her the following question:

'If these words had a sound, feeling or image, what would that be like?'
The result was:

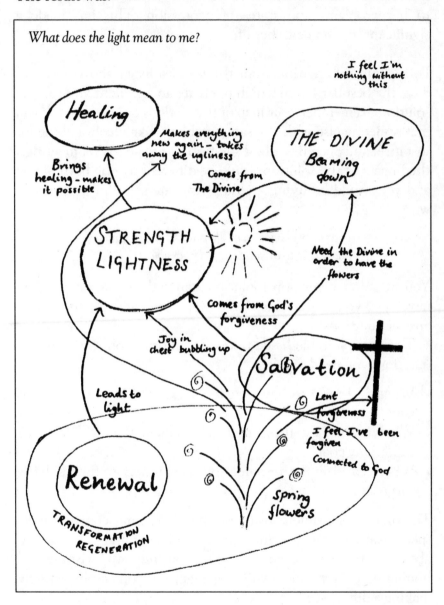

What does the light mean to me?

At this point Amanda had an obvious physical response to the map. Her face lit up, she smiled, her body relaxed and she said, 'Wow!' Amanda has been battling with clinical depression for years. After completing this solution map she found that she had some visual images that she could apply within her imagination to her problems and states of depression. This has made a significant difference to her life.

By seeking information from the sources listed above you will have the best data from which to create an excellent and specific solution. Remember your map of the world is unique. Even if you met someone else with the same problem, like alcohol abuse for instance, and even if the best solution was to go to AA meetings; the impact of the solution would be different for the both of you and you would be living and applying the solution in different ways.

> *Your only obligation in life is to be true to yourself*
> *Being true to anyone else is impossible.*

You are going to develop a solution map in the same way that you developed your initial Emotional Map. You are going to ask and answer questions!

To gather suitable 'issue-resolving' information these are the questions you need to ask:

- What do I need to have, create or experience to resolve this issue?
- What is the best thing that can happen that will lead me toward my goal?
- Where can I find a resource that is appropriate for resolving this issue?

This may seem time-consuming, but it is time constructively spent. Rather than wasting time by worrying and complaining about the problem at hand or idling your life away wishing and hoping that the problem will just disappear; you can be actively making a difference.

Whatever resource you gather it is important to *apply* and *relate* it to the *information* on your Emotional Map. Once you have done the groundwork this method of problem solving is almost effortless. Allow your unconscious mind to do the work for you. Avoid your natural tendency to 'try hard' or to 'try to make sense of this'. Your forced efforts and desire to be logical will create a barrier for *organic change*. If you feel that you 'need to do something' go back to Chapter 13 and practise the exercises. This will keep your conscious mind busy while your unconscious mind gets on with the job of re-coding your programmes and re-installing beliefs and behaviour that are more appropriate and constructive for you now.

24   Evolving solutions

You are in an environment that you are so familiar with that you don't pay it any attention. What we are doing is helping you to become consciously aware of the unconscious. This unconscious is your metascape (*see* Chapter 21). Navigating your way through it is a bit like being in Alice in Wonderland. Reality is never quite what it seems and anything can happen!

Moving from problem to solution in your metascape is a bit like participating in a treasure hunt. To get to the goodies you have to follow some basic rules:

- You have to know that you are looking for treasure
- You have to follow the clues – regardless of whether they make sense or not
- You must stick with the metaphor and the information on the map
- You must record everything you experience
- You must avoid interpreting the information (Alice didn't!)
- You must ask 'What does this mean to me?' or 'What does this represent?' a lot
- You must affirm that you are seeking the best solution to your problem

Sometimes a solution appears spontaneously, as in Thea's experience (*see* Chapter 25). However, more often than not, you will need to leave at least 24 hours for the information on your first Emotional Map to gel. If you can, put your map on the wall (I hang mine between the kitchen and sitting-room so I walk past it often). Hold in your mind the question 'What do I need to have, experience or create to resolve this issue?' and carry on as normal. The question will be priming information that will lead you to a solution – this will take time, hours, or even up to a couple of weeks.

At the point where your unconscious knows, you will accept and act on the information. You will get the message and you will know what to do next. Trying to force the issue won't speed up the result, it may retard it in fact. If you experience frustration, anxiety, apathy, despondency or fear, go to Chapter 18 and read it. Do Multi Level Reading exercise 'Breathing Light', keep focused on the question 'What do I need to have, experience or create to resolve this issue?' and 'What's the best thing that can happen that will take me towards my goal?' You will get a result.

If you get stuck or you think you're doing something wrong, don't give up! Ask every question in the *Questions* section which follows, one at a time if necessary, until you get an answer. Particularly those on the 'gather and clarify information' list. There will be a response, even if it's only 'I'm tired', 'I'm fed up', 'What on earth am I doing this for?' and 'Nothing's happening.' Remember, you can stop and take a break and come back later.

When you've gathered your resources, you need to ask 'Is there anything else?' and then 'What's the best thing that can happen now?' If no major change occurs, ask 'Can this happen now?' and 'What needs to happen before change can occur?' *then* 'What's the best thing that can happen now?' Keep asking these questions until you know you've completed your solution map.

We have scrupulously reproduced both a resource gathering session and a solution map to illustrate the methods, and the points we have just mentioned. This is an opportunity to see with your own eyes the pleasures and pitfalls of Emotional Mapping. It shows that while you are learning the technique it is important to follow the instructions to the letter. When you do so, success and resolution is inevitable. You may recognize some of your own behavioural patterns here. However, because each experience is unique, one person's solution will not be in anyway a solution to your issue. You still have to do your own map! Read it thoroughly, it will save you time and energy later.

You will need:

- A training map or large blank sheet of paper – A3 sized is best
- A surface on which you can spread yourself out
- Sticky tape
- Coloured pens and crayons
- Something to write with
- A comfy chair – make sure you can place both feet flat on the floor

Or

- A favourite piece of floor – with a wall on which to rest your back
- Cushions, a rug or blanket
- Some uninterrupted time – set your answerphone and switch off the phone please

Before you start please do a five-minute focusing exercise of your choice. Then read the Multi Level Reading exercise in Chapter 14.

Close your eyes. Have the issue you're working on in mind and mentally state your intention to find a solution. Then ask, '*What do I need to have, create or experience in order to resolve this issue?*' Write or draw the first unconsidered response to that question on your map, like so:

What do I need to have, create or experience in order to resolve this issue?

The information on the map leads to the next question.

This is the start of Harriet's second Emotional Map: 'A ☃ image flashed through my mind. I thought "That can't be right, what would I need a ☃ for?" So I checked it out and stuck with it.'

Harriet looked at the image and then asked: '*What does ☃ mean to me?*' She drew the answer on her map like so:

What do I need to have, create or experience in order to resolve this issue?

Something *FUN* you can do with *COLD*

The information on the map leads to the next question.

Harriet needed more information about her last answer, so she asked, '*What is* (FUN) *communicating to me?*' She drew the answer on her map like so:

What do I need to have, create or experience in order to resolve this issue?

Laughter
Playtime
Community games...

Something FUN
you can do with
COLD

The information on the map leads to the next question.

Another useful question to ask if the information you are receiving is vague might be '*I need more specific/practical information.*'

The images were beginning to give Harriet some insight. She then asked of her last answer, '*What does* — Laughter, playtime, community games — *mean to me?*' The answer she got was, 'As long as I wrap up warm I can have as much (FUN) with people as I want.' She drew the answer on her map like so:

What do I need to have, create or experience in order to resolve this issue?

WRAP UP WARM!!

Something FUN you can do with COLD

Laughter Playtime Community Games...

The information on the map leads to the next question.

She then asked the map, '*What does* 🐌 *mean?*' Her answer was 'protect myself'. At this point Harriet got confused. Both this map and the last one were telling her she needed protection. Looking at both her maps she asked, '*What question do I need to ask next?*' The question that came to mind was, '*How can I protect myself and still have* (FUN) ?' In response, she got an image of water, which she then drew on her map, like so:

She then asked of her map, '*What does* (WATER) *mean to me?*' Her answer was 'The snow needs to thaw.' She drew this on her map, like so:

At this point, Harriet started getting frustrated at herself – she didn't know what to focus on next. Sometimes, when an issue is particularly relevant, the answers can be:

- Very powerful and uncomfortable and you might not want to look at them
- Elusive – because you don't want to look at them!

With practice you can learn to tell the difference between an issue that *can't* be answered yet because the timing is wrong, or an issue that you *won't* look at because it is too threatening. Either way, the solution is to hold the issue in mind, go into your sanctuary space and from your sanctuary breathe light with the issue in mind. Wait a couple of days before tackling it again. Keep a note pad by your bed as you might have some interesting dreams!

When Harriet came back to her map after a short break, she was able to start afresh and look at the information in front of her in a new way. 'As much as I want to receive practical information as to how to resolve my issue, the information I seem to be receiving is all in metaphor and trying to make sense of it has left me confused, bemused, frustrated, feeling useless, like "I can't do it" and I just ended up getting irritated. I forgot that when you receive an answer in metaphor, you *use* the metaphor.'

Of all the things she had written and drawn on her map, the image of (WATER) attracted her most. She asked of the image, '*In relation to my issue, what does* (WATER) *mean to me?*' The answer was instantaneous, and she wrote EMOTION on her map, like so:

The information on the map leads to the next question.

Having filled in all the bubbles on her map, Harriet looked at both her maps and began asking questions about the metaphors in front of her. Using the ☃ as her resource, she asked, '*I wonder what would happen if I took the ☃ to the 'small-vulnerable-me' (svm) image on the first map?*' She proceeded to carry this out in her mind and her answer was, 'When I took the ☃ to the **svm**, I became encased within the ☃. It felt very cold, but safe and I felt I could relax. The ☃ was covering for me.' She drew the results on her map, like so:

What do I need to have, create or experience in order to resolve this issue?

The information on the map leads to the next question.

She then said, '*I wonder what would happen if I* 🧎 *inside the* ☃ *?*' She was surprised by the answer she got, 'I'm not frozen any more, and I'm able to walk around with the ☃ as if I'm wearing him like a costume.' She drew this on her map like so:

> *What do I need to have, create or experience in order to resolve this issue?*
>
> Emotion
>
> WATER
>
> The snow has to thaw
>
> SMALL VULNERABLE ME safe inside snowman
>
> WRAP UP WARM!!
>
> Laughter Playtime Community games...
>
> Something FUN you can do with COLD
>
> The information on the map leads to the next question.

Again looking at the information on her maps, Harriet asked the question, '*What happens when I take this image to the* (WATER)?' After carrying this out in her head she responded, 'I jump into the water, the "costume" floats off and melts and I find myself swimming naked under water. I feel a wonderful sense of freedom.' She put the information on her map, like so:

The information on the map leads to the next question.

Because the metaphors on her map were so obscure and seemed to have no logical bearing on her original statement 'I would like a loving, committed relationship', it was difficult for Harriet to see whether or not she had found a solution.

However, the feeling she got from her last answer led Harriet to feel she'd reached some kind of completion with her map. Just to make sure, she asked of the last image, *'What's the best thing that could happen now?'* the image responded, 'I'm quite happy just swimming here for a while.' She then asked, *'What practical steps do I need to take to help me resolve this issue?'* The answer she got was 'Check on the image of myself swimming under water daily to see what happens next.' She wrote this on her map, like so:

What do I need to have, create or experience in order to resolve this issue?

The information on the map leads to the next question.

Several days later, after checking the image of herself swimming daily, Harriet noticed a radical change in her feelings, attitude and behaviour around relationships. She said:

> 'I realize that until now I've closed myself down emotionally, especially to people who consider themselves to be my friends. I suddenly feel like I want to open up more to people – start being a proper friend. I realize that my vulnerability *stems* from confusion when a relationship changes – for better or worse. Now I think change could be interesting. I also mistakenly thought that my friends had to be "perfect" because I felt their behaviour reflected on me. Whoops! I feel kind of restless. I want to get out more and expand my horizons. Although I am still a little fearful of intimacy I feel almost compelled to meet and get close to new people. Whatever next?'

Remember:
Sometimes, the information you seek can be elusive. You may need to ask different types of questions from the list below and formulate your own from the information on the map. You may also need to make several resource maps, or make the one you are using bigger.

Often, if you don't get an answer at all it is because you are fatigued or stressed out. Remember to rest, breathe and relax. Sometimes you may not like or believe the information you gather. Learning how to trust your unconscious can take time, patience and practice. If this is the case:

- Go back to Part 1 of Emotional Excellence. Spend time on the exercises in each chapter. Particularly relaxing (Chapter 1), focusing (Chapter 14), breathing light (Chapter 11) and the Multi Level Reading exercises.
- Practise Emotional Mapping and after each map breathe light for five minutes or longer.

Remember:
Gathering resources is part of a process that leads to a solution of your issue. The process will lead to a change in your attitude, behaviour or both. The change may be obvious or subtle.

Note:

Once you've gathered all your resources and put them on your map, you then need to ask What does this represent? or What does this mean to me? To conclude the solution process you will then need to ask 'Is there anything else?' and/or 'What's the best thing that can happen now?' These questions trigger spontaneous emotional shifts. You can experience a shift from a scale of 'nothing much happened' to 'Wow!' If you are uncertain as to whether you have completed the change process or if you feel stuck at this point ask 'Can this happen now?' and/or 'What needs to happen before change can occur?' Map the response. *Thereafter* repeatedly ask 'What's the best thing that can happen now?' and 'Is there anything else?' until you have a sense that the map and the change process are complete.

So, what are you waiting for? Just follow the instructions and go for it!

QUESTIONS TO ASK WHEN EMOTIONAL MAPPING

Self-discovery questions. These have been donated by trainee Emotional Mappers. You can use them to gain confidence with Emotional Mapping. Exploring these questions will help you to clarify your thoughts, beliefs and feelings on the subject under focus:

- What does love mean to me?
- What does success mean to me?
- What does money mean to me?
- What does health mean to me?
- What is it to be happy?
- What is it to be sad/depressed?
- What is it to be relaxed?

You will find the answers penitent, interesting and illuminating. They will help you to recognize which areas of your life need attention and may even lead to you asking more applicable issue questions.

The big issue

You can use these questions either when nothing seems to go right, and there is so much to attend to, when you are confused; or when you know that your life is out of kilter in some way and you cannot put your finger on what's wrong. They work well to allay fears, transform procrastination and prevent writer's block.

- What in my life requires special attention?
- What am I not paying attention to right now?
- What am I avoiding?
- What am I ignoring?

Start-up questions

- What would I like to have different in my life?
- How do I know there is a problem?
- What are the symptoms of the problems or issue?
- How can I gain clarity about . . . ?
- How can I rectify . . . ?
- How can I benefit by/from . . . ?
- What can I learn from this?

Lifestyle questions

- What actions can I take to stop smoking, drinking, needing, feeling, resentful, lonely, frightened?
- What actions can I take to start a new project, dieting, being successful, feeling more positive about . . . ?
- To make the best of my life what aspects require special attention?

Questions to gather and clarify information whilst Emotional Mapping. These questions keep the information flowing and will help you stay focused on the issue:

- What have I discovered about my issue so far?
- What does this image/feeling/sound/word mean to me?
- What question do I need to ask next? (Ask this whilst looking at this list of questions.)
- What is this information communicating to me?
- What is my body telling me?
- How is this relevant to my issue?
- Is there anything else?
- What does this represent?
- How can I experience this safely?
- What needs to happen before change can occur?
- Is there a pattern to my behaviour?
- How does this pattern express itself?

Questions to help gather resources for solution maps

- What do I need to have, experience or create to resolve this issue?
- What is the best thing that can happen that will take me toward my goal?
- How can the information on my map help me to form a solution?
- How can I best apply this knowledge to make a positive difference in my life?

Questions related to childhood
If you find yourself dwelling on childhood events or receive information about a child or children when Emotional Mapping these questions are really useful:

- What event or childhood belief requires special attention now?
- What aspect of my personality is damaged?
- What aspect of my personality is out of balance?
- How can healing occur?
- What does this child/baby need in order to grow?
- How can this child receive what it needs now?
- Can I experience this now?
- How can this situation be laid to rest?

- What is the best thing that can happen that will resolve this issue?

For seasoned Emotional Mappers

- How can I better develop the spiritual side to my nature?
- How can my unconscious mind work better for me?
- What am I?
- How can I build a better relationship with my family?
- What is my purpose in life?
- What is my vocation?
- What does life mean to me?
- What does death mean to me?
- How can I live to my true potential?

A question of habit
Obesity:

- What does nourishment mean to me?
- What am I hungry for?
- What is appetite?
- What is lacking in my life?
- What is the benefit of my excess body fat?
- What do I have to swallow?

Smoking:

- How do I use cigarettes/tobacco?
- What do I need to express?
- How can I have more room to breathe?
- What is the pattern to my smoking?
- What does security mean to me?
- How can I gain clarity in my life?

Alcohol:

- What do I have to swallow?
- What sorrows am I drowning?
- How do I abuse alcohol?

- What does alcohol mean to me?
- What is lacking in my life?
- What is the pattern to my drinking?

When seeking information that leads to resolution of your issue

- What would my higher self say or do?
- How can my unconscious mind help me now?
- In what area of my life have I experienced success?
- How have I achieved these results?
- How can I re-create this successful behaviour now?
- What thoughts, feelings or beliefs do I have that lead me to success?
- How can this information help me toward a solution?
- What skill do I have that I can apply to this situation now?
- What skill do I need to learn to make a positive difference to this issue?
- What is the best thing that can happen that will resolve this issue?
- How can I be more responsible for achieving my outcome?
- Do I know, or know of anyone who does this successfully? (One mapper uses characters from *Star Trek*, another asks 'What would a Jedi Master do?')
- Can I experience this now?
- How can I emulate their behaviour?
- How can I apply that skill to this situation now?

These are questions for those times when problems arise between yourself and others. They will usually be related to an event, misunderstanding or error of judgement.

- What happened?
- How do I feel about what happened?
- How can acceptance help?
- How can I mend or correct the situation?
- What would have made a difference?
- What insight have I gained from this experience?

- How can I ensure a better outcome next time?
- How can I bring love and trust into this situation?
- What is the best thing that can happen that will resolve this issue?

TROUBLESHOOTING

Below you will see a table listing common statements, problems, quandaries and situations that may arise when first learning Emotional Mapping and when you engage in a programme of personal growth. Whenever you have a question simply read down the listings on the left-hand side of the table until you find a sentence that resembles your query. Then look at the column to the right. There you will be directed to either a chapter, or an exercise in this book that will help you to resolve your enquiry.

Question	Solution
I don't know what question to ask to get started.	For ideas and guidelines go to Ch. 20 Questions . Then look at Charlie's Emotional Map Ch. 28 Power. Do Multi Level Reading Ch. 5 Influential reading.
I don't know what to do next.	To become more familiar with the Emotional Mapping technique read through Ch. 22 to 24 for ideas.
I keep getting stuck.	You need more information and encouragement. Look at Poppy's map solution Ch. 8. Ch. 22 Emotional Mapping for beginners. Ch. 24 Evolving solutions – Questions .
This is difficult.	You need more information. Go to Ch. 22 Emotional Mapping for beginners. Ch. 14 Silence is golden. Ch. 5 Multi Level Reading exercise.
I am finding this process uncomfortable. I don't like what I am seeing. This is scary. My body hurts.	Read Ch. 2 A bit more basic and do Happy Thoughts exercise. Ch. 18 Trust and do the Multi Level Reading exercise. Ch. 19 Sanctuary. Ch. 21 The land that time forgot. Ch. 25 Love.

Question	Solution
This is tiring. I'm exhausted.	You may be trying to achieve too much too soon. Go to Ch. 15 The quiet mind.
I can't draw.	Emotional Maps are for your eyes only. You do not need to be a master draftsman to get a result. Relax (Ch 9 Basic Revisited) and remember to use lots of colour.
I can't get any images.	Practice makes perfect. Go to Chapter 16 Feeling thoughts. Chapter 19 Sanctuary. Ch. 6 Multi Level Reading Exercise.
My map is too wordy.	As above. Ask yourself 'If this word had an image sound or feeling what would it be like?' Then use shapes and colours to describe it.
This information is irrational and ridiculous. I keep questioning the validity of the information I am receiving. This doesn't make sense. This doesn't mean anything to me. This can't be right. The answers don't make sense.	You are analyzing the information. Remember you are working with metaphor. Read Ch. 21 The land that time forgot. Go through Ch. 16 Feeling Thoughts, and complete all the exercises. Ch. 13 Mastering the monkeys, including Multi Level Reading
I can't make head or tail of it. I can't get any answers. I don't understand.	You are thinking about the process instead of responding to the questions or the answers you have received. Read Ch. 12 It's all talk and Ch. 18 Trust. Do the exercises in Ch. 14 Silence is golden and Chapter 15 The quiet mind. Ch. 13 Mastering the monkeys.
I don't feel I can go on with this.	You may be tired, confused or fearful. Go to Chapter 15 The quiet mind. Read Poppy's Map Chapter 27 Money. Ch. 14 Multi Level Reading Exercise.
So many words, images, sensations and feelings have come up that I don't know which one to start with.	Ch. 14 Multi Level Reading. Refer to Thea's Maps Ch. 25 Love. Record everything you experience on paper. You may need lots of space. Of each image or word on the map ask 'What does this mean to me?' Take your time. Use Chapters 22/24 as reference guides.

Question	Solution
I think I'm remembering something that didn't happen. Could I have false memory syndrome? Is this a past life memory? How do I know whether my experience really happened?	Remember you are working with metaphor and representations. Go to Ch. 21 The land that time forgot. Read Chapter 19 Sanctuary.
I feel like I've opened a can of worms.	You may be attempting to move too fast. Take things one step at a time. Relax and meditate whenever possible. Go to Ch. 11 Multi Level Reading. Read Ch. 8 There is Always a Rainbow . . .
I'm feeling emotions I've not had before. I am tearful and I feel like crying all the time. I am really angry. I feel like an alien. I don't like myself/friends/life very much. I can't trust anyone any more. I am feeling isolated and lonely. I can't relate to my friends and family. My opinions have changed. One moment I feel great, the next terrible. My friends think I'm crazy. I feel like a basket case. I've changed, people say I'm very different.	These statements are very common. They are indications of transition and breakthrough. You may feel as if you are in no-man's land living somewhere between where you started and where you are going. This is a time for self-assessment. You may want or need to review your beliefs, values, principles, lifestyle and priorities. Refer to Ch. 25 Love. Ch. 18 Trust. Ch. 12 It's all talk. Ch. 19 Sanctuary. Read Ch. 28, Ch. 29, Ch. 30 and Ch. 31.
I feel tired all the time. I can't feel any emotion. I am not responding to my questions.	It's time to integrate and rest. Go to Ch. 15 The quiet mind. Do Happy Thoughts Exercise in Ch. 2 A bit more basic.
How do I know when I've finished my map.	Go to Ch. 24 Evolving solutions. Ch. 26 and read through Harriet's map thoroughly. Go to Ch. 29 Over to you and do Multi Level Reading. As you become more familiar with Emotional Mapping you will develop an instinctive feel for when you have completed and transformed an issue.

Part 4

25　Love

In the following pages we are going to take a look at the subjects that come up most frequently as points of concern in workshops and sessions. They are the issues and problems that you are most likely to discuss with, or hide from, a friend, and they fall into the four broad areas of love, sex, money and power. To illustrate each point and to encourage you to practise your training and use Emotional Mapping™ we have shown examples of issues that were being explored by clients at the time of writing this book. The subject under discussion was explored and brought to point of solution using the techniques outlined throughout this course. I cannot tell you how to solve your problems. I will, however, encourage you to explore your personal attitudes and beliefs. They are the only ones that count in your life!

LOVE

I have discussed love first because in the learning of it we learn about everything else. Contained within that one small word is a universe of experience and a world of possibility.

Before we can have love in our lives in its fullest sense we first need to understand its nature. Love is not just a word that describes how much you enjoy the taste of peanut jelly sandwiches. It is much more than a statement that describes the degree to which something has importance to us. Love is greater than the feeling we have for others that we care about. It is a force that governs the existence and evolution of consciousness. Think of it as the air you breathe. A never-ending all-encompassing force that flows through and around us. You express your ability to love when you do loving things for yourself and others. Love is something you encounter each time you allow thoughts from your imagination to take form. You can experience it when you bring something into being. This something may be new life, a piece of artwork, a project, a friendship, a dream brought to reality and more.

> *Art is a collaboration between God and the artist,*
> *And the less the artist does the better.*
>
> André Gide

We all learn about love through the experience of seeking love. Yet lost in the seeking we can forget the purpose and outcome of the lesson. This is to understand and appreciate the place life has in the universe and to know and cherish individuality while accepting and valuing unity.

> *The most common trait of all primitive peoples*
> *is a reverence for the life giving earth,*
> *and the native American shared this elemental ethic:*
> *the land was alive to his loving touch,*
> *and he, its son, was brother to all creatures.*
>
> Stewart Lee Udall

The message contained within the theme of love has been a muse to philosophers, storytellers and poets since man could talk. Here are some ideas for you to ponder:

> *To love is to receive a glimpse of heaven.*
> Karen Sunde

> *Love doesn't just sit there, like a stone, it has to be made, like bread; re-made all the time, made new.*
>
> Ursula Le Guin

> *Love is supreme and unconditional; like is nice but limited.*
> Duke Ellington

> *To fear love is to fear life.*
> Bertrand Russell

The way to love anything is to realize that it might be lost.
G. K. Chesterton

Love is the triumph of imagination over intelligence.
H. L. Mencken

The human heart is like Indian rubber: a little swells it, but a great deal will not burst it.

Anne Brontë

Love is, above all, the gift of oneself.
Jean Anouilh

Where love is concerned, too much is not even enough.
P. A. C. de Beaumarchais

I have found the paradox that if I love until it hurts, then there is no hurt, but only more love.

Mother Teresa

Love conquers all things . . .
Virgil

Love is a universal thirst for a communion, not merely of the senses, but of our whole nature, intellectual, imaginative and sensitive.

Benjamin Disraeli

So now you know.

Love is something that you will learn in degrees. It comes in a multitude of guises from joy and passion to fear and hate. Practising trust, acceptance, compassion and empathy make the lessons easier. When you allow for the possibility that everything you spend, regardless of its apparent or obvious meaning, is a lesson in love, you can make your experience loving. When you attend skilfully to the lesson right in front of you your experience of love becomes unconditional. You are open to giving and receiving what you want, and you will always have exactly what you need.

Life has its ups and downs. Love makes it easier.

Look up the words 'love' and 'hate' in the dictionary and thesaurus. Find at least ten words that you can add to your vocabulary to replace those much over-used words. Use the word 'love' only when you really mean it.

THEA'S EMOTIONAL MAP

'How do you know there's a problem?'

Thea: 'It has something to do with worthiness. I have difficulty accepting that I'm loved. It's very easy for people to say "I love you", but a lot of the time it feels like manipulation or fear to me. Even though I can't assume that anyone can know better than me what I need, I've spend most of my life waiting for people to give me what I couldn't give myself. So I think I want to look at how I can be more loving towards myself.'

This is not about a current behaviour, but about an experience Thea would like to have in her life. Therefore, the question she chose to work with is *'What is it to be loved?'* This is one of those profound questions that would benefit from Thea working from her sanctuary space.

1. Thea tuned into her sanctuary space. She asked her question and drew her answer on her map: 'It's like a tunnel made of sandstone lined with sand which feels soft underfoot. I'm walking towards a sandy space with waves, blue sky and sunshine.'

2. Thea asked, *'What does this mean to me?'* Her answer came immediately. She drew 'Freedom' and 'Release' on her map.

3. Again she asked the question, '*What does this mean to me?*' Her answer was 'Limitless space to breathe' and 'Open hearted'.

4. She then asked the question, '*What is it like to have limitless space to breathe?*' Her answer was 'Expansive' and 'Infinite'.

5. '*What does this mean to me?*' she asked again. 'Sharing and caring' was her response.

6. Thea had now filled in all the bubbles on her training map. Looking at the map, she asked, '*What have I discovered so far?*' She said: 'That I know how it feels to be experiencing feelings of love.'

7. '*Is there anything else you want to add?*' was the next question. She added the words 'Wonder' and 'Relief' to the rest of the information.

8. Following the instructions to the letter, the next question to ask was '*What is the thing that attracts you most?*' She pointed to

and said: 'The beach through the tunnel.' *Please note* that whatever attracts you on your map is fine. It doesn't have to be a whole image, statement or word, it might be a detail or a part of one.

9. Thea asked, '*What is the connection between the beach and . . . ?*' She drew arrows between

and every other image and word on her map, writing her answers across the arrows, like so:

What is it to be loved?

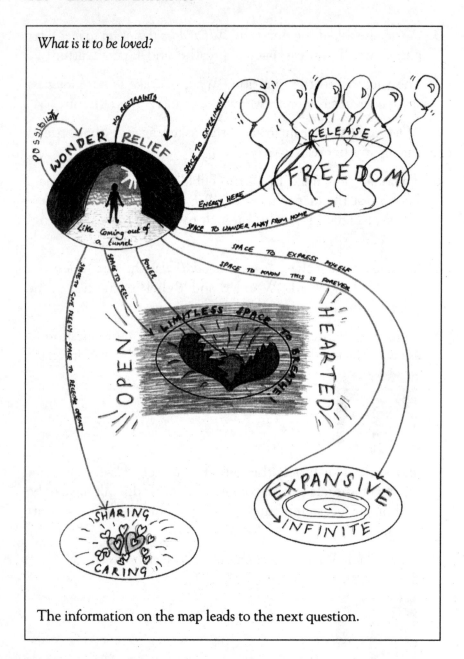

The information on the map leads to the next question.

10. And now another review. Thea asked, '*What have you discovered now?*' This is what she wrote: 'The first image of a tunnel was very vivid. I had a sense of mild excitement. The

sky looked very blue and I knew when I stepped out of the tunnel that it would be very hot and the light would be blinding. In response to all the other questions, there were enormous uplifting feelings. I can see by looking at my map that I really need to give myself credit for getting this far. I am surprised that I do not feel needy. The next step seems to be practising this feeling of SPACE in my life. I'm not certain how I can apply this but I know that having had a taste of it, I want more. I obviously need to uncensor myself!'

11. With her review in mind, Thea asked the question, '*Is there anything else to add to the map?*' Using a fresh piece of paper, Thea drew the following image:

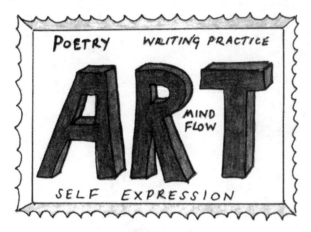

Now put the book down and do something completely different.

The solution

1. Having done this she asked herself, '*What question do I need to ask for a solution?*' She said, 'There was an awareness from doing my review that I censor myself and the only thing that prevents me from giving and receiving love in a way that's currently appropriate is to untether my mind and emotions. Without realizing it I had already asked, "*How can I do that?*" And what came up was the *art* image. Interestingly, I am aware that to express myself in this manner will take a degree of discipline!'

2. Having realized about the discipline factor, things started happening automatically. As she continued to draw and write on her third map, Thea had to backtrack to find out what questions were leading to the images coming out of her mind. 'What's coming out on my solution map seems to be coming straight from my subconscious in a very comical and artistic way! The questions that triggered off these images were *How am I going to express myself?* and *What will it take?* As I'm recording this information, I can see and hear myself expressing myself authentically. Now I'm really motivated to put it all into practice.'

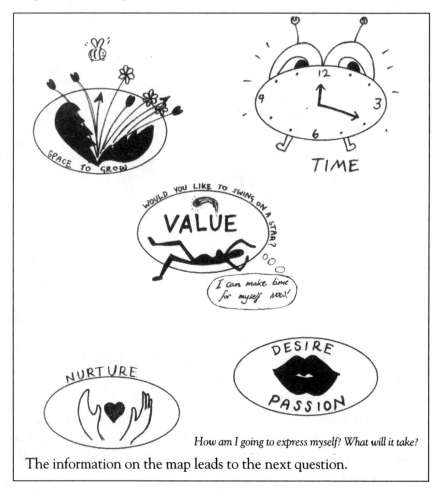

How am I going to express myself? What will it take?

The information on the map leads to the next question.

Here is proof that with Emotional Mapping it is not always the difficult beliefs and images that need to be uncovered in order to get to a desired outcome. It needn't always be uncomfortable. Thea's map shows us that this can be a very uplifting, enjoyable and amusing experience!

Here are some questions you may like to ask yourself about love

- What was I taught about love?
- How can I improve my capacity for love?
- What needs to happen before I can feel love?
- What needs to happen before I can give love?
- What was I told about love?
- How can I improve my loving relationships?
- What kind of loving relationships do I have?
- What's the benefit of my behaviour around love?
- How do I feel about myself when I don't have a loving relationship in my life?
- How do I express love?
- What do I believe about love? How do I talk about love?
- How will I know when I have enough love?
- What would it be like to have a loving relationship?
- How do I experience love?
- What does generosity mean to me?
- What does receiving mean to me? How can I express myself honestly?
- What is it to be a mother/father/daughter/son/sister/brother/wife/husband/lover?
- What statements do you have around love? Make a map.

26 *Sex!*

People spend more time thinking, worrying and agonizing about this one subject than any other. From the beginning of time people have assigned meanings to sex that go beyond the act of making babies. Sex and the expression of sexuality can become less about people and more about issues of right and wrong, status, ownership, attainment, performance, duty and obligation. Subsequently it has become a measure of our self-esteem and worthiness, prowess and potency. I find it unfortunate that an act so filled with the potential for expressing and receiving love and enjoyment, can be the cause of so many unnecessary bad feelings, misconceptions, abuses, problems, dissatisfactions and frustrations.

Attitudes toward it are often dictated by social, religious and cultural dictates and surrounded by doctrine. People who reject the endorsed line and step over it into the territory of socially aberrant behaviour run the risk of reprisals, reprimands, judgement, ridicule, incarceration, divorce and, in some cultures, even death. There is at once religious pressure to withstand temptation and religious pressure to go forth and multiply with the blessings of God. This dogma can be so rigid that even in extreme circumstances, classified by world health organizations as an emergency, like a starving nation endemic with AIDS, the official Vatican line is still 'do not use a condom'. How is it appropriate to condemn millions of people through fear and guilt to a debilitating fatal disease that can be passed to an unborn child? In this case perhaps the real disease is ignorance and dogma!

All life is driven to reproduce. Reproduction is sexual in nature. Sex is about attraction and allure. It has to be. You have to get close to exchange body fluids. For people sex has less to do with the physical act of copulation than we might realize and more to do with the emotions generated between partners. It is about communication, interaction and relationships and is at its best a trusting and intimate act of self-expression. Sex is not just about genital contact. It is about you and your whole body. You can have sex with or without affection – there are no rules about this. A good sexual experience is about pleasure and sharing. That means feeling good about yourself, your partner and what you are doing. It also means that you continue to feel good when you think about it later. You can make it loving, playful, lustful, fanciful, silly or serious. To have really good sex it is important to approach it with a degree of responsibility and planning. Bad sex is worrying about unwanted consequences. Sex is simply sex.

> *What closeness! Only the human animals*
> *join so close; heart to heart, mouth to mouth.*
> *See how that sets us apart so that it isn't only sex . . .*
> Susan Trott

Harriet's Emotional Map

'*Why do you feel the need to explore this subject?*'
Harriet: Because in previous relationships I have had difficulty distinguishing between love and sex and where they meet. Also I start feeling sick and very nervous when I think about broaching this aspect of my life, which is usually an indicator that something about this frightens me.'

'*What do you think your specific question might be?*'
Harriet: 'I think I need to ask "What do I believe about sex?"'

1. Harriet asked the first question '*What do I believe about sex?*' Her answer made her feel quite strange. "Gold pillars on a white background," she said.

2. She asked, '*What does*

mean to you?' and her answer came back, 'There's the sound of wind blowing over a Roman landscape.' Harriet has begun mapping straight from her metascape.

3. '*And what does the sound of wind mean to you?*' she asked. She wrote: 'Harsh', 'Abrasive' and

on her map.

4. '*And what does*

mean to you?' she asked. She saw an image of a girl with dark hair, wearing an elaborate costume of red and blue. She was sitting amongst rocks on the outskirts of the scene.

5. '*What does*

mean to you?' was the question. She wrote: 'Run away', 'Hide', 'Dejected' and 'Hurt' beside the picture of the girl on her map.

6. She asked herself, '*What does*

Run away

mean to you?' She drew an image of a bright green

containing a diamond on her map.

7. Harriet had filled in all the bubbles on her map and felt it was time to review her work. She said: 'I'm feeling very dizzy and there are intense feelings of pressure around where my heart is. I feel quite breathless. The information seems quite disjointed but overall there is a sense of loneliness attached to each image. There is a lot of fear about being hurt and vulnerable. I'm boiling hot and the way my body feels makes me realize that this is a very profound process.'

8. The next question was '*Is there anything else you want to add to your map?*' She added the words 'Vulnerable', 'Feel very sad' and 'Protection' where she felt they would be appropriate.

9. '*Out of all the things on your map, what stands out most?*' she asked herself. Harriet pointed to the image of

The next step was to connect everything on the map to this image.

10. *'What's the connection between*

and . . . ?' She proceeded to link

with every other word and image on the map with a red arrow, writing her responses across the arrows.

11. Harriet reviewed her art work: 'I'm getting the strangest information. It's like someone else's life story – this is nothing like my own life. I don't think I believe most of the beliefs

has about her life, but they came into my mind, so I put them down anyway. Because this is my metaphor, it must be about me! Protection seems to be the big issue here. The girl seems to need protection from a domestic situation of abuse that she feels she can't get out of. Where she is is all she knows –

for her, there is nothing else. I'm still very dizzy and hot. I feel like I could go to sleep now.'

12. She asked herself, '*Is there anything else you want to add?*' She wrote: 'Can't get out', 'Prison' and 'Bird in a gilded cage' beside

She also drew a picture of the way her body felt. Harriet's completed map looked like this:

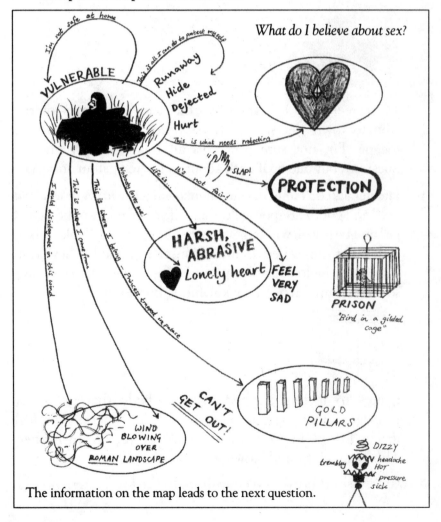

The information on the map leads to the next question.

13. Harriet reviewed her map for a third time. She wrote: 'The "Bird in a gilded cage" and "prison" metaphors sprung to mind and I suddenly realized that this was what the

were about. Just like a canary trapped in a bird cage, there is a feeling of desperation and resignation because

really feels she is trapped within the boundaries of the Roman town, yet she is always trying to find a means of escape. I'm not sure how this all relates to my original question, but maybe if I ask about it, I could get an answer.'

14. Harriet asked, '*How does this information relate to my belief about sex?*' and got the response: 'Because if you're going to be a good girl and be loved, you can't get out of it!' She said, 'I take this to mean that somewhere in my unconscious mind I believe that in order to be loved and approved of by a man I have to have sex with him! Oh no! That's awful! I also feel that

relates to feeling trapped inside a body that gives out messages about me that sometimes I don't necessarily feel inside. I think I need to take a break before I go any further. This is all a bit mind blowing really.'

Now take a short break and come back to the book later.

The solution

1. Looking at the list of questions, Harriet chose to ask herself, *'What do I need to have, create or experience in order to resolve this issue?'* In response, she got the song 'Follow the Yellow Brick Road' in her head, and an image of pathway leading out of the Roman town. She drew this into one of the bubbles on a fresh map.

2. She asked, *'What does this represent?'* And got the words 'Freedom' and 'Choice' which she wrote down on her map.

3. *'What does this mean to me?'* she asked again. 'Being let out of the cage' and 'Having a mind of my own' were her answers.

4. Harriet floundered a little, and then asked, *'Is there anything else?'* for want of a better question. She said, 'There needs to be a key.'

5. *'And what does a key like that represent?'* she asked herself. 'It opens the green heart!' she said with surprise.

6. She knew that she needed to ask a question which would enable her to do this, so she asked, *'What's the best thing that could happen now?'* In her mind's eye, Harriet saw a key fitting into a keyhole which had appeared in the green heart. The front of the heart snapped open as if on a spring, and as it did so, she saw hundreds of golden birds burst out and fly off. She drew all this information on to her map, like so:

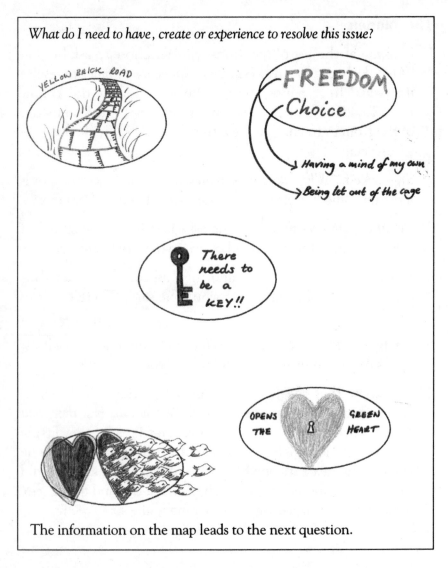

What do I need to have, create or experience to resolve this issue?

The information on the map leads to the next question.

7. She then asked again, '*Is there anything else?*' The answer was: 'The heart needs to be locked up again, and the key hung on a hook by the door.' Once she'd followed these instructions in her head, she now knew her Emotional Map was complete.

8. Harriet commented about what had happened: 'I know *something* happened because there was such a huge physical response. I almost jumped out of my skin when I saw the birds

fly out of the green heart like that! All at once I realized that the heart of the

was also the

which held the birds. I know that something has been released emotionally. I feel very peculiar, but have a sense that I'm free. I guess I'll just have to wait and see what's changed.'

Remember

Gathering resources is part of a process that leads to a solution of your issue. The process will lead to a change in your attitude, behaviour or both. The change may be obvious or subtle.

Note: Once you've gathered all your resources and put them on your map, you then need to ask 'What does this represent?' or 'What does this mean to me?' To conclude the solution process you will then need to ask 'Is there anything else?' and/or 'What's the best thing that can happen now?' These questions trigger spontaneous emotional shifts. You can experience a shift from a scale of 'nothing much happened' to 'Wow!' If you are uncertain as to whether you have completed the change process or if you feel stuck at this point ask 'Can this happen now?' and/or 'What needs to happen before change can occur?' Map the response. *Thereafter,* repeatedly ask 'What's the best thing that can happen now?' and 'Is there anything else?' until you have a sense that the map and the change process are complete.

Here are some questions you may like to ask yourself about sex:

- How do I express my sexuality?
- How does my current relationship affect my life?
- What's the value of being feminine?
- What's the value of being masculine?
- What is the relationship between sex and love in my life?
- What does feminine mean?
- What does masculine mean?
- What do I believe about sex and sexuality?
- What was I taught about sex?
- What is the benefit of my sexual behaviour?
- What kind of sexual relationships do I have?
- How can I improve my sexual relationships?
- How do my feelings about myself/my body affect my relationships/sexuality?
- How do I feel about myself when I don't have a sexual partner?
- What was I told about love?
- How do I talk about sex?
- How do I experience sex?
- What does generosity mean to me?
- What does receiving mean to me?
- How can I express myself more honestly?
- What is it to be a sexual partner?
- What is it to be a husband/wife/lover?

What statements do you have around sex? Make a map.

27 Money

Money it turned out, was exactly like sex,
You thought of nothing else if you didn't have it
and thought of other things if you did.

                                            James Baldwin

What is this stuff called money? Taken literally the answer to
that question can only be paper and plastic and pieces of
amalgamated metals. That's all it is.

During a workshop entitled 'Prosperity' we brainstormed the
question What is money? Here is the result:

It seems that money isn't just paper and plastic after all!

I wonder what would be the purpose of a life lesson in money? As a child it always seemed odd to me that those who had the most were always worried about losing it. Those that had a little more than enough always wanted more. Those that had just enough complained that they didn't have enough. And those that really didn't have enough were busily inventive and had many different ways in which to make ends meet.

Henry Ford sums up a lesson I had to learn when he said, 'If money is your hope for independence you will never have it. The only real security that a man can have in this world is a reserve of knowledge, experience and ability.'

Here are some quotes on money for you to agree or disagree with.

Lack of money is the root of all evil.
George Bernard Shaw

Money is not required to buy one necessity of the soul.
Henry David Thoreau

Money is the wise man's religion.
Euripides 425 BC

It takes as much imagination to create a debt as to create an income.

Leonard Orr

Money speaks all languages.
J. R. Ewing – *Dallas*

Taking it all in all, I find it is more trouble to watch after money than to get it.

Montaigne

Money is that which brings honour, friends, conquest, and realms.
John Milton

And forgive us our debts as we forgive our debtors.
The Lords Prayer

Man was born to be rich or inevitably to grow rich through the use of his faculties.

Ralph Waldo Emerson

Money can't buy me love.

The Beatles (amongst others)

All my investments are profitable, either in money or valuable experience.

Jerry Gillies

The safest way to double your money is to fold it over once and put it in your pocket.

Ken Hubbard

Poppy's Emotional Map

'*How do you know there is a problem?*'
Poppy: 'Nothing I do works out.'

'*What are the symptoms of the problem?*'
Poppy: 'Lack of money mainly. It effects everything.'

'*What is everything?*'
Poppy: 'The way I live, how I relate, self-image. The way I tackle problems – I don't have any enthusiasm.'

1. Because Poppy had made a statement: 'Nothing I do works out' we then chose the question '*What's it like to be lacking?*' and Poppy's immediate response was

After a few 'What does this mean to me?' questions and responses, Poppy's initial map looked like this:

What is it like to be lacking?

The information on the map leads to the next question.

2. At this point, there were a lot of words to work with, but not many images which could make the map more difficult to decipher later. Poppy asked, '*Is there any image or colour you want to add to your map?*' She responded, 'It's just the way I feel. The feelings in my body seem to be overwhelming

everything else.' 'What do those feelings mean to you?' Poppy said, 'They mean I'm vulnerable.' She circled the word on her map so it stood out.

Remember to put down *everything* that comes into your head, however ridiculous it seems, and use as much imagery and colour as you can.

3. Poppy then asked, '*Of all the information I have gathered, what attracts me or demands my attention the most?*' She said, 'I'm drawn to

So now we made

the central point on the map and asked the question '*What's the connection between disempowered and . . . (every other image and word on the map)?*' She drew an arrow with her answers between

and each image/word on the map.

4. Poppy then reviewed the map for a few moments. She said, 'I've felt the response in my body most strongly, I feel numbed out from my solar plexus upwards. My headache is getting

worse and I feel sick. The bottom half of me feels totally separate. I am surprised that the word

now feels more like 'being attacked'. I would certainly do this again because of the immediacy of the process.' Poppy wrote any extra information she had gathered from her review on the map.

5. At this point Poppy is becoming consciously aware of the unconscious information she has gathered. She looked at her map again and asked, '*Is there anything else you want to add?*' This can include body sensations or feelings, any questions, thoughts, sounds and imagery. Poppy added some more words and images to her map like so:

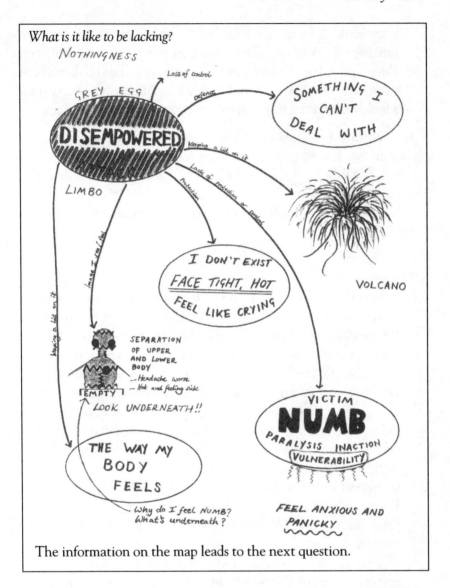

What is it like to be lacking?

NOTHINGNESS

GREY EGG

Loss of control.

DISEMPOWERED

Defence

Keeping a lid on it

Lack of protection or control

SOMETHING I CAN'T DEAL WITH

LIMBO

Protection

VOLCANO

I DON'T EXIST

FACE TIGHT, HOT

FEEL LIKE CRYING

keeping a lid on it

Image I see/feel

SEPARATION OF UPPER AND LOWER BODY

— Headache worse
— Hot and feeling sick

EMPTY

LOOK UNDERNEATH!!

THE WAY MY BODY FEELS

VICTIM

NUMB

PARALYSIS   INACTION

VULNERABILITY

Why do I feel NUMB?
What's underneath?

FEEL ANXIOUS AND PANICKY

The information on the map leads to the next question.

6. She reviewed her map again. 'I feel quite dizzy and light-headed. I'm also exhausted. I wonder why I feel anxiety and panic? I seem to have moved away from 'disempowered/attack' to focus on my body response. I realize that the feelings I'm experiencing are predominant over any thoughts or images I'm getting and I'm finding it difficult to ask myself

questions. Asking myself 'Why' doesn't give me any answers, but asking 'What's underneath?' might be more productive. I'm surprised at the feelings that came up as I did this exercise; normally my response would have been defensive or to attack. I feel I've taken a step towards finding answers to my lack.'

To facilitate integration of your Emotional Map and replenish your energy levels, go back to Chapter 9 and do the stretch/relax exercise. Then read the Multi Level Reading exercise described in Chapter 11.

Now put the book down and do something completely different.

The solution
1. When Poppy went back to her map after a few hours she saw it from a new perspective. She said, 'I looked at the questions I'd written on the map and began by asking "What is underneath?" I got an image of a page which I couldn't turn over. No matter what question I asked about this image I couldn't get an answer, so I decided to focus on something else. I then looked at the picture of the body. For want of a better question I asked "*What is my body attempting to communicate to me?*" and got the answer to look below at the "empty" place beneath my waist.'
2. Concentrating on the area between her belly-button and feet, Poppy asked, '*What is underneath?*' She got an image of a pregnant woman lying amongst green leaves which she drew on a fresh map.
3. She then asked the question '*What does this mean to me?*' In response she got the words 'Primitive and natural' and added 'Motherhood is really important to me.'
4. She asked, '*What does "motherhood" mean to me?*' and wrote the responses 'safety' and 'nurturance'.
5. Looking at what she had just written, Poppy said, 'But I haven't got any safety in my life.' She then asked the question, '*What needs to happen for me to experience safety in my life?*' The

answers she got were 'I have to trust and be vulnerable' and also 'Giving birth'.

6. Poppy asked, *'How can I trust and be vulnerable?'* Her immediate response was an image of a baby. She drew all this information on her map like so:

What is underneath?

PRIMITIVE
NATURAL

PREGNANT BELLY AND BREASTS

MATERNAL...

SPOTLIGHT
MOTHERHOOD IS REALLY IMPORTANT TO ME

NURTURANCE
VULNERABILITY

BEING PROTECTED, BEING LOVED

HOW CAN I GET IT?

Safety

I HAVE TO
TRUST AND
BE VULNERABLE

GIVING BIRTH

LOVE

TO HAVE ALL MY NEEDS MET

DISEMPOWERMENT (LACK OF CONTROL)

BE OPEN TO IT / BE DISCERNING DEFENSELESS

TO BE PROTECTED LOVED

IN A PLACE OF SAFETY

EMOTIONS. I DON'T REALLY KNOW ABOUT LOVE

VULNERABILITY

HELPLESSNESS

INNOCENCE

EMPTY—
Failure...
lack...
guilt...
HAVEN'T GOT IT

RECOGNISE AND IDENTIFY
MY NEEDS

When can I experience this?

I NEED
TO
BE LOVED !!

The information on the map leads to the next question.

7. She asked the question, '*What does*

   mean to me?' She answered, 'Emotions – well, I don't really know about love.' She wrote this on her map. Having filled in all the bubbles on number two, Poppy knew that the next question should be '*What does the*

   need in order to grow?' Her answers again were 'Safety, nurturance and love'. She then went about making connections between the

   and love, safety and nurturance on her map.
8. Poppy asked a few more questions of her map, but felt she was getting nowhere. She then did a review. 'I realized my body was not responding to questions. I was exhausted. I had got so far with the map and seemed to have got stuck and was going round in circles. The answers I was getting kept referring back to my needing love and safety. I realized I was analysing the words and images and trying to relate them literally to my situation instead of using them to gather more information.'

What actions do I need to take for the baby to grow?

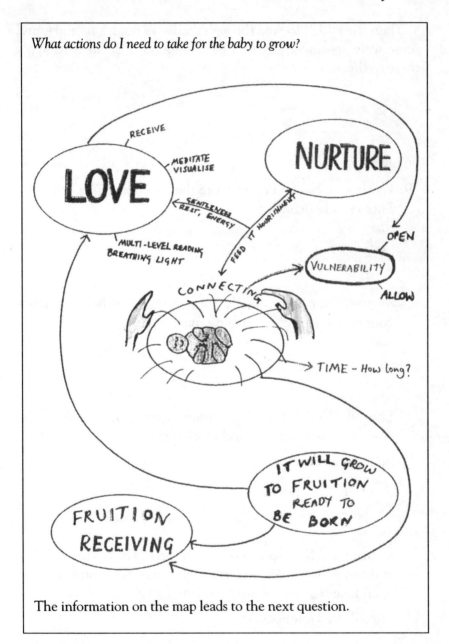

The information on the map leads to the next question.

Then she said, 'I looked through the list of questions and found some were specifically geared to childhood. I decided to apply these to the

on my map.'

9. Using a fresh map Poppy wrote the question *'What actions do I need to take in order for the*

   to grow?' She immediately got the image of healing hands connecting to and nourishing the

   She asked, *'What does this mean to me?'* and received the answers 'Love, nurture, and receiving.'

10. She asked, *'How can*

   receive this?' She received the answers 'Trust, vulnerability and time'. *'What does vulnerability mean?'* she wondered. 'Be open to and allow love' was the immediate response.

11. She asked, *'How does the*

need to experience love?' and drew the answers 'Feed it – gentle, nourishment, rest, energy, meditate, visualize, receive, breathe light, Multi Level Reading.'

12. '*And what will be the result?*' she asked.

'

will grow to fruition ready to be born.'

13. 'I knew at this point that I had come to some kind of conclusion as to how I could solve my issue,' Poppy said. 'Obscure as the information was, the instructions to myself were very clear. The question "*How long do I need to do this?*" came to me. I decided to sleep on it.

The following morning I woke up with a terrible backache. I remembered that for the last two to three months my body had been swelling up, particularly around my belly. I did think it possible that I could be pregnant! I also remembered that about ten years ago a friend had told me to find a photograph of myself as a baby and send it love – I didn't know what she was talking about at the time! It all seems to fit. The path ahead has been dark and dingy, but is now lit to show me the way forward.'

Although Poppy found her Emotional Mapping experience difficult to decipher at times, she always remembered to go back to the information in front of her and refer to the questions she had available. In this way she found the insight into her money issue and the solution to it tremendously useful.

As Emotional Mapping gets directly to the heart of the problem you may find that an issue which starts out being about one thing can later turn out to relate to something else. In the same way that a fever is often a symptom of an infection, your real issue may be masked by a habit or behaviour such as smoking or shyness.

Poppy was to discover that her lack of money was a *symptom* of a much deeper problem. Even though she found her Emotional

Mapping experience difficult to decipher at times, she persisted and always remembered to go back to the information in front of her. Whenever appropriate she referred to the questions she had available (see below and Chapter 24). By resting when she was tired and allowing time for the information to 'brew' she realized that her money issue was really about lack of love. Poppy resolved to listen to and put into practice the suggestions that her unconscious had outlined. Although challenging, Poppy found the whole experience extremely useful. Shortly after completing this map her life began to turn around for the better.

Here are some questions you may like to ask about your relationship with money:

- What was I told about money?
- What is the value of money?
- How can I improve my finances?
- What do I believe about money?
- What is the relationship between work and money?
- What needs to happen before I can have more money?
- What does wealth mean to me?
- How do I talk about money?
- What's my current financial status?
- How do I feel about money?
- What would it be like to be wealthy/abundant/prosperous?
- What does abundance mean to me?
- What is it like to be responsible for earning money?
- How will I know when I have enough money?
- How do I experience money?
- How do I believe about making/receiving money?
- What does generosity mean to me?
- What does it mean to receive?
- What does it mean to give?

What do you believe about money? Make a map.

28　Power

Some time ago I took a course which was being held on a university campus in London. During my time there I had the opportunity to meet a diversity of people that I would not otherwise have come into contact. As I think about the issue of power one young woman in particular comes to mind. Her name was Mary. I first noticed Mary in the student canteen. Every day for a week she sat alone behind a shield of books. Munching on nuts and crackers from a Tupperware box she cautiously observed the crowds of hungry, talkative students milling around her.

One morning I arrived on campus early. I had time to burn before my lecture so I got a cup of indistinct watery liquid from the coffee dispenser and took it to a table in the lounge. My head was buried in a book of poems when a voice quietly said 'hello'. Mary was standing elfin-like before me. She had been watching me for days, she said, and thought I looked interesting. We swapped information on courses and tutors. I gained some sorely needed tips about campus protocol and we went our separate ways. This was the first of many lunchtime meetings. Mary was the youngest daughter of a pastor and had lived all her life in a sheltered Christian community. She had a thirst and interest in history that always made for interesting conversation and had a refreshing perspective on past and present events that was obviously coloured by the custom and observance of her lifestyle. I often wondered at her certainty and conviction. Had she been born a hundred years ago she would surely have been a missionary.

The autumn was drawing to a close and with the holiday season looming Mary asked what I was going to do over

Christmas. 'My son has his barmitzvah next spring,' I said. 'We are forgoing the usual festivities for a traditional Chanukah this year.' 'You're Jewish!' Mary said in shock as she almost fell backward off her chair. I, somewhat surprised by the strength of her response, nodded in silence. Mary's cheeks reddened. 'Oh, I didn't realize. I'm sorry,' she said. 'I didn't know.' 'Are you sorry for your response or sorry for my faith?' I asked, smiling. Embarrassed, Mary looked at me and confessed: 'I have never known a Jew before.' I was curious and said, 'Does it make a difference?' Mary lowered her head. 'I don't know,' she whispered, her voice trembling. I took Mary's hand. 'Faith is a powerful thing,' I said reassuringly, 'it has the strength to heal, but also, it seems, the ability to drive a wedge between friends.' I looked into her eyes questioningly. 'You have an opportunity to live up to the power of your faith right now. You can choose to believe your prejudice or you can choose to believe your experience. I was born into the Jewish faith. It is a culture I enjoy, full of history and tradition that I respect. If I label myself as a Jew I separate myself from a Christian, a Muslim, a Sikh, a Hindu, an atheist. I have made a choice to see myself as a person linked to, and like, every other person. As to my faith, certainly I see it as something of value, just as you see yours. I am a person who practises some of the traditions of my forefathers. To me,' I said, looking her directly in the eye, 'tradition can give a sense of continuity, it is powerful because it can be used as a stabilizing influence in a changing world. However, tradition is not the whole world.'

Both our worlds became a little bigger that day. Our conversations became richer and often more heated. We began to study together. Our essays were often controversial but we always got great grades!

Mary and I continued to lunch together. We talked long and often heatedly about history and the hunger of insecure and avaricious leaders bent on taking power from others. It seemed to me that they had all missed the point. Power is not a quality that we can gain at the expense of another. Talking of having power in this way only leads to others trying to get it back. Here rests the cause of all human conflict, wars and revolutions. Real power is about choice. Choice is something that everyone has. It is not solely within the confines of those who have positions of power. Choice is a power that grows within a person as he or she develops the ability to make flexible and responsible (response able) decisions about the mutual strengthening of relationships. The more choice we allow ourselves the more choice we allow others. Thus power becomes an empathic self-generating force that bonds people together in self-respect, tolerance and love.

Charlie's Emotional Map

'How do you know you've got a problem?'
Charlie: 'Because it keeps happening.'

'What do you mean by "it"?'
Charlie: 'I end up in some sort of conflict with my work managers.'

'What kind of conflict is conflict like that?'
Charlie: 'Totally opposing views.'

'Do you have totally opposing views to everybody?'
Charlie: 'No.'

'So is this something that comes up only in the work place?'
Charlie: 'I have this with my father too.'

'Taking that information into account, what is the issue you would like to explore?'
Charlie: 'Er . . . I think it's something to do with authority.'

'OK, taking that information into account, what is the issue you would like to explore?'
Charlie: 'I don't know how to explain it. Authority represents being put into boxes for me.'

'OK, you are giving me a lot of information. What would happen if we just explored what authority means to you?'
Charlie: 'Could do – I'd probably get intellectual about it, though.'

'What could be the benefit of exploring what authority means to you?'
Charlie: 'Why do I keep getting into situations with people who are in positions of authority. What happens, why it matters.'

'Think of a statement or question about authority that you'd like to work with.'
Charlie: 'I always get stuck in how to formulate a question on where to start from.'

'OK. Go to our list of prepared questions and modify one. Keep the goal in mind when you are looking through the list.'
Charlie: 'OK, I want to take tension out of my working relationships.'

'Good. Now what is the issue or question you want to explore?'
Charlie: 'Ways to decrease or remove tension out of my working relationships.'

'Write your statement on top of the map. OK, what's next?
Charlie: 'I need to make it into a question. How can I . . . ?'

'Are you comfortable with that question?'
Charlie: 'Yes.'

'Charlie, just relax and tune into your bodymind. Ask yourself the question and put your first authentic response. Remember to take into account any thoughts, body responses and images.'

Well, by now you have seen that people can find it difficult to devise a first question. Charlie put up a lot of resistance to getting started and gave intellectual answers rather than responding to the questions. Sometimes it can be useful to work with a friend who will remind you of the 'rules of the game' and steer you in the right direction when your mind begins to stray. Now Charlie was able to begin mapping on his own.

1. Charlie asked himself the question on top of his map, '*How can I decrease or remove tension from my working relationships?*' He received several words and images in response, all of which he drew onto his map like so:

How can I decrease or remove tension from my working relationships?

The information on the map leads to the next question.

2. He asked of himself each word and image in turn 'What does this mean to me?' Again he received a huge amount of information which he wrote around each bubble, like so:

How can I decrease or remove tension from my working relationships?

The information on the map leads to the next question.

3. Charlie now reviewed his map and what he discovered was this: 'There are not many pictures on my map or many colours. This does seem like quite a stark issue, not very picturesque or colourful at all. From what I have written, I

realize that I perpetuate the tension – the barrier and flight/ fight syndrome is a tense reaction. I go into "war" mode, which means I react rather than respond to a situation. I physically act out my thoughts – I meet the tension with "tenseness" so that there is impact, rather like two tanks colliding, rather than holding my own and letting the energy flow over me. Could this match my weight problem? No wonder I didn't find a question easily . . . this reaches every corner of my life! This has taken about 15 minutes to do. It's so quick!'

4. Using all the information gathered, including his review, Charlie asked, '*Is there anything else to add to the map?*' He added the words

PHYSICAL

RESPONSE

in the last bubble on the map and wrote: 'This reaches every corner of my life, not work alone.'

5. The next question was: '*Of all the information on the map, what stands out most?*' His answer was BARRIER. Charlie now went about connecting each separate piece to BARRIER with an arrow, asking the question '*What is the connection between BARRIER and . . . ?*' like so:

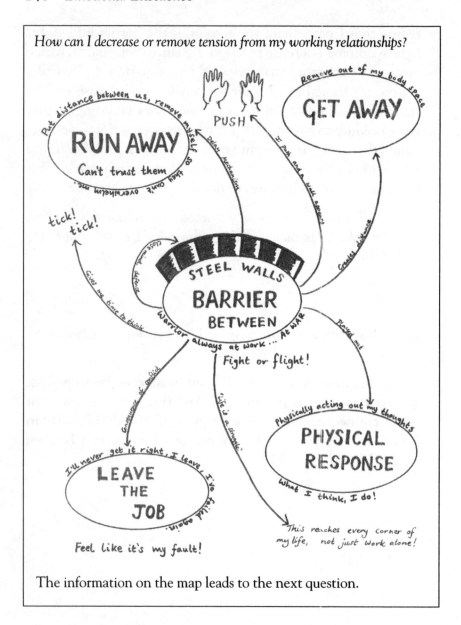

How can I decrease or remove tension from my working relationships?

The information on the map leads to the next question.

6. Now Charlie reviewed the map again. 'The paper isn't really big enough. I will need to do this again on A3. I'll have to work with a friend to discuss it because I tend to edit my own responses. It was difficult to put my thoughts into written words. This hasn't necessarily clarified the issue any further,

but it has made what I've already discovered more solid. I need to take some time out to integrate what's happened before continuing.'

Charlie went out for a while and on his return he commented, 'I've wondered about how I find life a struggle for some time, but I didn't know how it operated before. I started by wanting a solution, but I've had to face the behaviour first. Facing myself is always uncomfortable, but also a relief because realization works like a pressure cooker for me. Looking at the map again, I'm finding it hard to decipher all the words – I wish I'd used more imagery.'

We decided to leave the solution map until tomorrow, since Charlie felt he had already found out enough for one day.

Now put the book down and do something completely different.

The solution
The next day, he wrote down his thoughts as follows: 'I redrew the map on to a larger piece of paper last night, and began to get more pictures in my head as a result. The pictures were of my childhood and decisions I made around an incident that happened when I was three. I woke up worrying about money this morning and also a little scared. All this is a sign that I'm ready to go ahead with the solution map. I had trouble with the intensity of feelings I was experiencing, although the information on the map seemed not to be a part of me, but somehow detached. I'm pleased that I slept on this, and didn't attempt to solve the problem all in one go. It is too important, and I needed to feel and observe yesterday's discoveries.'

7. To help him find a resource for change, Charlie began with the question 'What is it that I need to have, experience or create in order to resolve this issue?' The response he got was straight from his metascape and he drew it on a fresh map, like so:

What do I need to have, create or experience to resolve this issue?

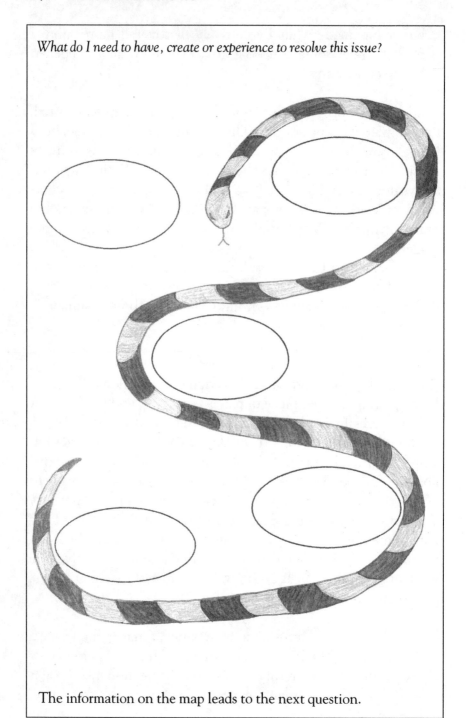

The information on the map leads to the next question.

8. The next question was easy. *'What does this represent to me?'*
He got an image of going into work with the imaginary

coiled around him. The snake took the form of an advocate
(rather than a defence) whereby negotiation could take place
with people in authority.

9. The next question he asked was *'What needs to happen before I
can experience this?'* Charlie was surprised that the

image appeared to talk to him. It said: 'You don't need the

any more. You need to decide how it comes down.' Charlie
asked, *'How does the wall need to come down?'* He got an image
of a big blue giant with a mace, bashing down the

on the first map. At this point, Charlie felt he had come to
some kind of completion with his issue. In his metascape, the

had been razed to the ground and he realized for the first time he could see clearly in front of him. He felt supported with the snake wrapped around him, and the big blue giant stood behind him for extra protection. He drew all the images on his map like so:

The information on the map leads to the next question.

10. He reviewed his solution map. 'I always worry that I don't know what I'm doing and I'll get lost, which would mean getting stuck with the problem for ever. The process was actually very easy, as long as I stayed with the questions and answers, rather than drifting off on a tangent. Just working with the pictures and trusting that they were right allowed me to move through this very swiftly. At the end, I had to check that I had actually exited the metascape properly. Even though I know I am back in the here and now, the snake still feels very reassuringly present.'

Charlie found his experience at work to be quite different during the next few days. He said he was extremely talkative and felt quite friendly. 'I looked up

in Medicine Cards (a system for divination and personal insight based on Native American tradition teaching the healing 'medicine' of animals). It means "transmutation and shedding of the skin". I can't sense the

any more and I felt less tense. There was a slight feeling of disbelief, but I did feel different.'

Part 5

29   Over to you

A word in your ear before you continue with this course. As you have come this far I am happy to assume that you have acquired some useful pointers by reading this book. Possibly you have discovered that you didn't need to read all of it? Maybe you think that the words and ideas are all well and good but that they do not apply to you. Perhaps you wanted more of something or needed less of something else. However, you have benefited up to this point and whatever you believe you are looking for, I will remind you that you will not find it in these pages. This book presents you with study material. It may be full of ideas, techniques and suggestions but it was not designed to teach you anything. This book cannot teach because everything you need to know and everything you want to learn is right inside you.

When the student is ready the teacher appears. Look in the mirror. Look at your life. You are your own best teacher. You know exactly what it is that you are attempting to learn about. It is at the forefront of your mind. It is under your nose or perhaps even under your skin. Right now you are busy living life to an agenda all your own, making up your mind, coming to conclusions and creating your own solutions even as you read. You are living it. When you are presented with a lesson to learn from it is ultimately you that makes the decision about what in that lesson applies to you. Only you can decide whether it is relevant or not. And you will know that only by the value that you place on things and the meaning that they have for you. And that is exactly as it should be.

One man's meat is another one's poison

A problem is something that goes round and round in your head. It is like a snowball rolling down a slope. It gathers more and more power and size with each revolution and the larger it gets the more momentum it seems to carry and vice versa. A question becomes a problem when there is a conflict between what you want, need or experience and the beliefs that you have about the consequence of having it. This is nothing new. Balancing wants and needs has always been a social and moral challenge for mankind. Now more than at any other time in history we are all in the throes of a revolution. This particular revolution is unlike any other that we have had to confront. It has its roots based firmly in technology and science and we are therefore faced with issues and inventions that are changing the fabric and status of our lives with every breathing moment. In changing and challenging times personal and social values can become vague and indistinct. The questions raised by so-called progress stretch many of the principles we were taught and expected to live by. We can and do lose sight of who and what we are. This is not an excuse for itinerant behaviour. It is simply a fact of life.

> *Every problem or quandary that you have stems from the disparity*
> *between what you actually believe and what you want to believe*

Throughout the Emotional Excellence programme you have had an opportunity to find out more about your beliefs and values. As you do so you can move, with a little effort, beyond the 'I can cope', 'I can't cope' see-saw of conviction, uncertainty and confusion that can mar your life and undermine your emotional confidence.

This process is dynamically beneficial in the long term and, as you will have discovered so far, it does have its immediate rewards. However, initially you may experience a degree of uneasiness. Reality can seem stark as you come face to face with it. You may unveil some uncomfortable truths about yourself and discover some disagreeable facts about your life of which you were unaware or had ignored before.

Now I know that the mere thought of facing up to the games

that *you* play can leave you cold. Right? This can be scary and confrontational. Everyone feels this way to one degree or another, because people are more used to giving and receiving mis-information than hearing the truth. It is not that folk deliberately walk around trying to deceive each other. It is just that saying what's on your mind, getting things off your chest, declaring your beliefs, and broaching issues and thoughts of a personal nature can be particularly difficult. At times like this communication can be particularly selective. In the short term it seems so much easier to use, or invite, undue compliments, diplomacy and tact. If we express an 'honest' opinion we could feel unsettled and intensely guilty or embarrassed if our words or intentions are misunderstood.

Let's face it, fibs, untruths and fabrications are a commonly accepted antidote to the fear of rejection or disapproval. And so what? What if our communication is often contrived and orchestrated? Why not make life a little easier? If it makes someone happy I am all for it. Just remember the words you hear may be a selective opinion. The 'facts' you hear may not be 'the truth the whole truth and nothing but the truth'!

Beauty is in the eye of the beholder

What is truth anyway? There are very few absolute truths. An absolute truth is something constant and unchanging. Like 'night follows day' for instance, or the 'moon orbits the earth'. On a personal level truth is always relative. The bedrock of your truth will be grounded in your culture, experience and expectations. Although it's important to you, in a global sense it is merely a viewpoint or a position based on conditioning and tradition. Your 'truth' may, or may not, depend on relevant facts and information. All truth is subject to a change in perspective and opinion. History books can be rewritten, memory is selective, political agendas change and scientists make discoveries. To the early Europeans America didn't exist. The world was considered to be flat with the sun revolving around it. Those who thought otherwise were considered subversive blasphemers. Now we know different. America is a country of worldwide influence and if someone insisted the world was anything less than a round rock hurtling through space we would call them mad or stupid. Wouldn't we?

> *Ideas, ideas, ideas. That's what we need*
> Helena Rubenstein

New ideas begin on the periphery of society. First they are ignored. Then they are rejected. Then they are denied and attacked. If they hold water or are relevant to society then slowly, slowly they make inroads until finally they are acknowledged and even accepted. After all, slavery has been abolished, women gained the right to vote, education is accessible and free from segregation, and native culture is valuable and wise.

In the natural world, before new growth is seen, there often has to be a letting go, a pruning of dead wood, a thaw in the ground and the ground may be especially prepared. The same can be said of you. You too will need to sweep up the leaves, cut back the brambles and clear out the cobwebs in your metascape to be free of lazy or outdated beliefs and behaviour. It is this clearing that makes room for the new. In a way it is a little like removing junk from an attic so that you can build a loft. During the process you will find things that you haven't seen for a while. It is amazing how many dusty boxes can be stored away in the recesses of your mind without you noticing. There they are piled high one on top of another. The sight can be overwhelming and off-putting to say the least, but take heart. Amongst all the rubbish there is certain to be a treasure or two. You may need to empty the boxes though.

As you work your way through your storeroom of thought you can expect, for all the reasons and examples outlined in this book so far and many, many more, to find vast discrepancies between what you actually believe, what you think you believe and what you want to believe. You are not going mad! This is normal. Every person I know lives with conflicting or paradoxical beliefs and behaviours that lie around in their mind playing an unconscious game of tug of war. We only seem to notice when all that tugging pulls us toward somewhere, or keeps us in a place where we would rather not be. When you want to make a permanent and lasting change to your life, you will need to find out which of your thoughts or feelings hold you back and which move you forward. Then you will need to decide which you want to keep and which you need to dump. Sometimes this can be a tough decision. To help yourself take appropriate action you can ask the following questions. How does this idea serve me? Does this belief lead me toward my overall goal? You will know what to do by the answers you receive.

Take the best, leave the rest

Take a positive action right now. Make yourself comfortable. Set the answerphone to pick up your calls and put a Do Not Disturb sign on the door. Stretch your body and take some deep breaths until you feel that you have let go of some of your mental clutter. Now just sit down, either cross-legged or with both feet flat on the floor. Begin by reading the following passage slowly and rhythmically, pausing for breath at the end of each sentence. Remember you can gain some benefit from reading this passage, and you can gain a different benefit by committing it to tape and then listening to it with closed eyes.

I would like you to discover something. Now I do not really know what you might discover but I do know that you can be curious about what that something might be? You already know that you can change a sensation within your body just by paying specific attention to it. You have spent time learning how you hold a book and you have influenced the pace of your breathing just by counting. As these words bring those memories to mind what can you notice about your mind and your body right now? How does reading about the skills you have been learning prompt your memory and what are you remembering? How can

these questions help you to discover something? What is it like to wonder in this way? As you think about all these things you may also notice how your thoughts can be here and somewhere else at the same time. Thoughts can come and go as you read. Some thoughts may be relevant to the words on this page while others may drift in and out of your awareness without you knowing why? What thoughts can enter your mind whilst you sit and read while other thoughts can drift away? How do your thoughts change as you breathe and discover new images in your mind? Did you know that you can, by running your eyes over these words, simply exclude from your mind any thought that you do not need to be aware of right now? In all probability you will shortly discover that you can lose a thought that you no longer need. At the same time you can also discover in your own special way how to retain thoughts that are happy and useful. It may be that you already know how to liberate a thought that has outlived its usefulness. Maybe you are about to find out? What would it be like to find new and useful thoughts replacing any outdated ideas? I want to remind you of something you already know – your mind is a unique and special place, isn't it? Now I can tell that it's good to know that there is a special place that can attend to all your needs. I am certain that your mind knows how to listen to a useful thought. What kind of questions do you need to hear now? I do not know for certain what you are experiencing. However, I can see that you are experiencing precisely what you need in exactly the right way. Now listen to your breath. Take a deep breath now. Remember how to 'let go' as you exhale. Be aware that there has been a change in your level of relaxation. Your chest can rise and fall as you use your breath to help you integrate new learning into your everyday life. What kind of thought is like a belief? What kind of belief can serve you for the best? How could you best benefit from updating some of your beliefs? Take a deep breath now. What can happen as soon as you choose to 'let go'? What's the very best thing that can happen now? Would you be willing to experience that in your life right now or do you need a little more time? How soon can you experience it and discover the many benefits in your own way?

In an interesting way you can discover how a special place can store special memories. It's so easy because your mind knows these things. As you discover what you need you can recall a time when you felt so good. And as that memory comes to mind, it can be interesting to discover that at exactly the same moment you can give up some part of a memory that is no longer useful in your life. I wonder how you did that? You have discovered so much and still I would like you to discover more. Perhaps you can begin to notice that whenever you have a good memory learning something new becomes very easy. Have you begun to notice yet that learning is an agreeable experience? What is it like to experience an agreeable learning experience like that? How can you learn to recognize a belief that you no longer need? What question will help you to develop new and useful beliefs? Let it come to you without thinking about it, like happy thoughts come to mind. It appears that your unconscious mind can be intent upon your highest good. Very likely it already edits and erases thoughts that are of no benefit. Your mind knows many wonderful things about you that you are just beginning to find out. I can remind you now, that you have discovered in your mind, a vast place where you store many things. And your unconscious mind can enable you to explore these places in your own time. If you wish you can call upon an inner explorer who really enjoys seeking out positive outcomes to all your queries and questions. It is so nice to know that you can easily discover more and more ways to do things easily. You can easily count from one to four and recall that rhythmic breath. If you wish you can either relax deeply now or just take a few moments. And as your inner mind decides, you can take deep rhythmic breaths as you read the words on the page. You already know how much benefit you can receive from a rhythmic breath that flows through your body in this way as you breathe in and out. As you finish this paragraph you can find yourself closing your eyes to take some time to sit quietly and integrate new realizations as this rhythm flows through your body like a stream of light. You will know when it is time for your eyes to open. And it will be easy to remember how to seek positive outcomes. And you can really feel the benefit of taking the time as you come to full waking awareness once again.

Be aware of the room around you now and focus on your feet. You can feel the floor beneath you. Now focus on your feet and as you feel your feet flex and wiggle your toes. Stretch your body. Breathe in deeply and blow out hard. And again breathe deeply in and blow out hard. Be ready to *stretch your body and open your eyes*. Look around you. What colours can you see? That was an interesting exercise. Well done. Clap your hands hard together for a few moments. Great. Now for something completely different.

30   *Help yourself*

The spirit of self-help is the root of all genuine growth in the individual: and, exhibited in the lives of many, it constitutes the true source of national vigour and strength. Help from without is often enfeebling in its effects, but help from within invariably invigorates.

Samuel Smiles 1859

To have anything you must either see or recognize the value of it. It is through knowing the value of a 'thing' that you decide, either consciously or unconsciously whether you want it or not. Now I can see hands raised to heaven and hear protesting voices saying, 'Oh, but I want money and I'm always broke.' 'I want a good relationship but somehow things never seem to work out.' 'I want a good job but I'm stuck in this position.' Via my own experience and by helping others navigate through theirs, I can honestly tell you I know that what you say is true and that your current standpoint is sincere.

Now what I am about to say may seem either alarming or could be something of a relief. Remember the words on this page express my perspective. Currently this is focused on a number of social habits, attitudes and preferences. They are presented here for your consideration. You can toy with the ideas as you deem appropriate.

More than ever it has become acceptable (at least in psychoanalytical and therapy circles) for individuals to abdicate responsibility for their current dissatisfactions and problems by shining a spotlight on 'stuff' that they experienced in their past. It is tempting, when things aren't working out, to find relief through self-justification and a belief in mitigating or extenuating circumstances: 'Well, you know my father beat me! My mother didn't care. I lived in a real rough neighbourhood. School was —— and I just don't want to talk about that thing that happened when I was twelve, OK?'

Each one of us has a script. So, what happened to you? What is your story? Like it or not, the inevitable (and empathic) response is,

'THAT'S LIFE!'

The very fact that you were born (and still resident on planet earth) means that from time to time shit can happen. Really good things can and do happen too. When you look at the fact that there's a choice, doesn't it seem absurd that so many folk (elect to) take the damaging 'stuff' to heart then hold fast to it as if it were a life raft in a stormy sea. How is it that so many people spend so much time convincing themselves that life is a struggle? Not content with that, they then compete with others to prove that their life has been the hardest. 'You don't know you're born. When I was you're age I had to scavenge for coal.' 'What a luxury, when I was young we didn't even have a hearth!' To me this kind of emotive dialogue sounds (and usually feels) like an attempt to control others either by guilt or blackmail – 'I worked so hard you had better appreciate it' or 'I'm so exhausted, if you don't help me out I'm going to die.'

In one way or another each of us has been open to the inevitable effects of emotional coercion. This occurs because people are more inclined to prioritize external demands above their own internal requirements. Through fear of showing need or weakness they proudly overlook and decline help from others while performing amazing acts of martyrdom – especially where work, status and money are concerned. However, as the saying goes 'No man is an island'. The consequence of all that self-denial is that people begin to feel unappreciated, taken for granted, anxious, put upon, resentful, misunderstood, angry, tired, under the weather, accountable or scared. The result is often a series of symptomatic emotional diseases like stress-related illness and breakdowns in relationships.

What's really going on here is a cry for time and attention. The attention being called for is:

'LOVE'

My preferred definition of love, is that it is the giving and receiving of appropriate attention. To be attentive one must give mindful and observant attention. To attend appropriately (to yourself or others) requires that you have regard for the likely consequences of your efforts. Think of it like this. Love is like water, people are like plants. All need an optimum amount to flourish. Too little water, we withdraw and wither, too much and we drown and stifle in good intent.

Neglecting your intrinsic emotional needs is a careless act of self-deprivation. To wallow in self-indulgence is a wanton act of emotional gluttony. Both are acts of self-imposed cruelty. Life is full of paradoxical extremes but it need not be in interplay of opposites. Nothing is ever black and white – except black and white of course. It is not a matter of which is better. Each can be applicable when considered and offset against different colour schemes (areas) of your life. You are free to paint your days in a spectrum of unrestrained colour. This, if you like, can include multiple shades of grey.

Remember within the heart of your emotion you will find see-saws, slides, swings and roundabouts. When it comes to living (especially the loving bits) I believe in fun and balance. What goes up, from time to time, must come down – so long as it goes up again later!

> *Oh, I'm so inadequate – AND I love myself!*
> Meg Ryan

As an advocate of the proactive and positive approach to self-help I have reservations about psychotherapy and analysis as a method of self-healing. It seems to me that for lack of love (and in an attempt to find it), people will justify spending years and years (and huge amounts of money) in therapy or psychoanalysis. What concerns me is that during the process (which in some cases may be three or more times a week and last for years), the client is encouraged to look back, usually to times of sadness and distress in order to feel better about themselves. They pay (often dearly) for the privilege of reliving their trouble, pain and strife – not once, but again and again. To me this looks and feels like hell on earth!

Now, one of the 'life-skills' you have become aware of during this course is the power of the bodymind connection. It's a fact that when you 'think bad' you 'feel bad' and vice versa. It is also true that wherever you focus your attention (whether this is your thoughts, your time or any other kind of energy) you will achieve the most concrete result. What do you think will happen when you focus on past experiences that were painful and frightening? What occurs if you perpetually replay mind movies of events that went badly for you? You will automatically and unceasingly relive those feelings and re-create those experiences – they may not be identical but there will be enough similarities for you to begin to notice the patterns. With these facts in mind what makes you think you are going to feel good when you are focused on feeling bad?

> *The mind is its own place, and in itself can make heaven of Hell, a hell of Heaven*
>
> Milton

Yes, I know that there are always two sides to any coin, so for argument's sake, let's look at the benefits of seeking to understand the past (as opposed to the benefits of therapy). Standing back and taking an alternative perspective on events and behaviour can be useful as it may:

- Help to alleviate distress
- Calm and dissipate anger
- Reclaim self-esteem and confidence
- Give you a sense of control
- Help and encourage you to repeat past success – this is good

Now, the tricky thing about this process of gaining understanding is that it can become the goal, the result to aim for, rather than being seen as a stage in our journey from which we continue to grow and evolve. When this happens it may unwittingly:

- Become a crutch or a mask which hides a more authentic you
- Inhibit you from moving on to new pastures
- Be a justification for defiance, complacency, despondence and depression
- Be an excuse for self-defeating habits
- Lead to a belief that a situation that you live with or a habit that you do is permanent
- Develop into a reason or an excuse not to change
- Show you exactly how to replay unsuccessful behaviour

I rest my case. Prior to moving on – and before I put any more noses out of joint – I concur that there will always be exceptions to any rule. In the short-term, any method of self-exploration is useful and healthy, particularly when it stretches the boundaries of one's beliefs. It takes courage and commitment to turn your life around. There are so many people, disadvantaged or otherwise, who do good, make good and contribute to the lives of others. To all of you – and you know who you are (some will have benefited from 'doing' therapy!) – I say a heartfelt congratulations.

The most extraordinary fact about the past is that people worship it

Returning to the subject of the past – realistically, anything that has already happened lies in the part of your mind reserved for memories. It's gone. It's over. It's finished. That is as true of any event that has happened. Even the words you read just a moment ago are a memory. They are consigned to a storage place in your brain. Within your consciousness they can be as up-close or as distant as you need them to be. The information will be available to you only when you require it. It is not necessary to recall every event in your life simultaneously – that would be silly or confusing (or worse!). Your mind thinks and remembers in sequence.

We have talked about memory in previous chapters. You know

that it has particular qualities. It has a selective capacity and it can change. All your memories, and therefore the effect that they have on you, will alter in some way over time. This can happen as a matter of course or you can productively modify them to suit your needs. To make my point try this. As you are reading don't think of a sunset. It is easy to know what a sunset looks like because you have seen one before. It's likely that the harder you try not to see it the more vivid it will become. So, as you have a sunset in mind you may as well make the best of it. Now, in some way modify the image so that it becomes more attractive to you. You may change the colours or the quality of the light. You could make it bigger, brighter, deeper. What about sound? As you adjust it watch it change even as you watch the sun sink below the horizon. See how the stars begin to appear? If you like you can close your eyes for a few seconds. Good. Now you really understand by your own experience that you have a built-in ability to amend and embellish anything you choose to.

By means of an image we can wipe out pain and lighten up pleasure

Human beings are so flexible. Each one of us can readily adjust to changing circumstances. When times are good we will eagerly expand our horizons, bank balance and in some cases our waistline. In times of unemployment, homelessness, poverty, social conflict, famine, war and unprecedented 'acts of god' (which we all unfortunately either hear about, or may experience directly) people learn to adjust. This is called 'a survival strategy'. Considering the likely state of affairs it is a good tactic. Living becomes about making ends meet, tightening belts and keeping your head down. In extreme circumstances life can seem like one long endurance test. Amnesia sets in. People may be so concerned with 'staying alive' that they impassively settle for less than they want or really deserve.

I only want enough to keep body and soul apart
Dorothy Parker

For fear that things could be worse they cope and learn to tolerate their present circumstances and dream about tomorrow. Despondency grows, dissatisfaction follows. You can hear it in people's voices when they talk about the situation. 'I've had enough. I ought to throw in the towel. I'm tired of waiting for something good to happen. What's the point anyway? Nothing changes. It's just not fair.'

Rather than being disenchanted or in a recurrent state of disappointment you can take your frustrated expectation and turn it around. For every action there is an opposite and equal reaction. The flip side of despondency is motivation. Have you noticed just how 'fed-up' some people need to get before they will make the decision to change? That tiny statement speaks volumes. It says 'enough is enough!' It means 'I can't take any more.' 'I'm up to here with it.' At this point people are so full of the 'it' (whatever that might be) that the problem becomes intolerable. It is too much to bear. Something has to change! 'Fed up' is angry and frustrated. It's like steam building up in a pressure cooker. If left to its own devices it can either implode – which basically means you will turn your frustration in on yourself and perhaps take drugs like alcohol, nicotine or worse, have a breakdown, or create some life-threatening illness and be too damn tired to fight it, get divorced and watch your life fall apart – or you can remember that all emotion is energy (remember Chapter 4). Regardless of its quality it is powerful and vital. It is a force that when used dynamically will get you moving in any direction you desire – other than the one in which you are currently pointed in that is – and shape your life for the better.

If you are unhappy, if the shoe doesn't fit, if 'it' could be better, recognize and own it. Be dissatisfied. Your mind will quickly get the message and all too soon you will be 'fed up' to the eyeballs. Even though you may feel aggravated and restless this is a powerful time. Take advantage of it. You are preparing to break open your shackles (self-imposed or otherwise) and you are generating the energy that will free you. Whichever way you look at it, one thing is for certain, however tough or boring life gets times do change for the better – you can try to deny it but that's the way life is.

The most self-empowered way to have what you want is to be happy about it. Whatever you already have and whatever you want to acquire you will enjoy it to its fullest when you have a grin on your face and a smile in your heart. Happiness like any other feeling is a state of bodymind. It comes and goes.

How could you intensify a feeling of happiness? Imagine that you can relive the very best moments in your life. Look at the words listed below.

Exhilarated	Overjoyed	Intoxicated
Vigorous	Animated	Lively
Energetic	Stimulated	Elated
Turned-on	Euphoric	Ecstatic
Loved	Joyful	Empowered
Wonderment	Dazzling	Wild
Excited	Sexy	Passionate

What would it be like to re-experience them now?

Exercise ✍

Choose a question from those below.

- What is it like to experience . . . ?
- When was the last time I experienced . . . ?
- How does it feel to be . . . ?

Then randomly pick a word from the list above. Ask yourself the question adding the word you have chosen at the end. For example, how does it feel to be dazzling? Using a bodychart to record your responses ask the following questions in turn:

- Where does this feeling start?
- Where does it go?
- Where does it end up?
- How can I intensify it?

> *When a fantasy turns you on,*
> *you're obligated to God*
> *and nature to start doing it*
> *— right away*
>
> Stewart Brand

The best thing about that exercise is that it is seductive. Every evocative, alluring, wonderful, memory leads to another and another. You can experience exhilarating, powerful feelings which intensify and intensify until they all merge together. You might end up with a cocktail of pleasure. You could fill a flask with it. What would it look like? What about liquid gold or fluid light? What happens when you drink it down? How does it spread through your bodymind? You could bottle it and take it into your Sanctuary? It is just so powerful. The more you use it the more its potency increases. You have a never-ending supply. What could happen when you apply it to dull and lifeless areas of your life? You may want to use a paintbrush, a spray gun, a hose or a sprinkler system. Where can this fantasy lead you? Add a few drops to that river of tears and that ocean of despair. Watch. How does the energy expand as it dissolves into the water. Use your imagination. Would you like to make it even better? Just think, it could be all pervasive. Honestly, it could filter into and influence every area of your life as easily as you want it to. It can do anything you dare to dream.

> *If it has value take it to heart. One must not lose desires.*
> *They are mighty stimulants to creativeness, to love and a long life.*
> Alexander Bogomoletz

I sometimes look at life like a game of snakes and ladders. Like the roll of a dice, a chance event or meeting can take you up a level or two. But why leave it to chance? If you want to succeed, and by this I mean achieve your ambitions, you need to know what your goal is. You should also be aware of its location both literally and in your metascape. Then when its time to make a move take your dice, focus on the outcome, be determined to aim for it every time. See it, crave for it, feel ecstatically good and happy about having it. And as you throw those dice across the board keep them in your sights and the end result in mind. (Incidentally, what is it like to have goals like yours? What can you tell about your desires? When did you last take a look? How can you clarify them? Is there anything that could make them feel even better?)

If you do find that you 'slip' back to your old habits, roll with the punches. You need not tolerate a situation that isn't in your best interest. Remember how bad it was at its worst. Refuse to accept it. Recall that frustration, and create enough of that 'fed up' to break free and then lose the image. Refocus your attention on your goal. Bring back the motivation, the pleasure and the excitement. Intensify it, make it bigger, make it brighter, wrap it around yourself. Thoroughly experience the feelings. Keep your eyes on the prize, take a determined breath and throw those die again.

When the going gets tough the tough get going

Take a positive action right now. Make yourself comfortable. Set the answerphone to pick up your calls and put a Do Not Disturb sign on the door. Stretch your body and take some deep breaths until you feel that you have let go of some of your mental clutter. Now just sit down, either cross-legged or with both feet flat on the floor. Begin by reading the following passage slowly and rhythmically, pausing for breath at the end of each sentence.

It may be that as soon as you see this typeface you antici-pate a change in the pace of your breathing. Now I would like you to have a new kind of relaxation experience. What would need to happen for you to have the very best re-laxation experience you could ever have? What is it that you can do right now that will make all the difference? What changes need to occur and how soon can they happen? How can reading this text help you to have a really good experience like that? What is happening to your breath now? How does your body feel? Do you notice any changing sensations and what might they be? How does this experience surpass any other relaxation experience you have bad before? How can it be even better now? What kind of relaxation develops deeply in this way? What can happen to improve it now? I do not really know how

you are feeling but I do know that you may still relax a little bit more as you observe a deeper and deeper developing comfort within your bodymind. Only you can find out how it will feel to be as relaxed and as comfortable as you can possibly be. Now listen to your breath. If you feel the need take a deep breath now. Your chest can rise and fall as you recognize that there has been a profound change in your level of relaxation. I don't know if you are quite aware of these changes yet but as you begin to notice that your mind can wander you can continue to find out. Throughout this book you will have read many thoughts and ideas. A seed is like an idea. You can seed a thought and be curious as to what can grow from it. You have worked very hard clearing and preparing the ground to yield a harvest. Now you can take the time to look into your metascape and discover your inner garden. And where might that garden be? Is this garden like your Sanctuary or is it completely different? As you find yourself in this natural place what season have you found? In nature a seed will germinate in the growing season. Throughout the cold season a seed may lie dormant for some time. Even as it sleeps a seed will somehow know that with the change of season it can spring to life. And it can wait and wait and wait until the conditions for growth are just right. I wonder what seeds you have planted? How can your garden grow?

Now I know that in exploring your inner landscape you have come a long way. A long way can seem like a distance, but a distance may take no time to travel. You can journey into your past and imagine yourself being there in a moment, and you can picture yourself in the future as if you were there right now. Then again there can be occasions when time, rather than rushing by, can be on your side. When you take a life-long journey for instance. Sometimes, you can have so much fun and so much pleasure that you will experience every moment as valuable and precious. So precious in fact that you can want to take it to heart and treasure it there. And as you look inside you may find a pearl of wisdom or a jewel of an idea and simply feel compelled to share it with others. It is so difficult to contain excitement, it is one of those things that bubbles up and radiates for all the world to see. You know that you can admire beautiful things and you can see that many other people will admire beauty too.

Now, as you travel you can meet so many interesting people and see so many inspiring things that you can be enthusiastic about. You can move between one place and another with an aim in mind, taking all the time necessary to discover what you need. As you journey on your way you can be certain that your destination is waiting patiently for you. There are so many different ways to travel and so many routes you can take. You may prefer to go by foot or to pedal on a bike. You might want to drive or fly or sail or swim. Perhaps you'll decide to tread water for a while. Who knows? Who knows? I certainly don't but perhaps there is a part of you that understands there is a value in not knowing everything. As you go on your way, I wonder how you will discover the value of uncertainty? It is a very special state of mind. Perhaps you are sceptical about that? Being sceptical is a little like wondering. And as you wonder it is such fun to be curious about what can happen next. An inquiring mind can be open to a series of delightful surprises, and a surprise can be like an opportunity. Now, remember that wherever you travel and however you take your journey you can be sure in an uncertain kind of way, that you will arrive at exactly the right place at precisely the right time to make the best of any opportunities on offer. So as you wonder what they might be you can take a deep breath and refocus your attention in the room around you.

Be aware of the room around you now and focus on your feet. You can feel the floor beneath you. Now focus on your feet and as you feel your feet flex and wiggle your toes. Stretch your body. Breathe in deeply and blow our hard. And again breathe deeply in and blow out hard. Be ready to *stretch your body and open your eyes*. Look around you. What colours can you see? That was an interesting exercise. Well done. Clap your hands hard together for a few moments. Great.

> *There are seasons, in human affairs, . . . when new depths seem to be broken up in the soul, when new wants are unfolded in multitudes, and a new and undefined good is thirsted for. These are periods when . . . to dare is the highest wisdom.*
>
> William Ellery Channing 1829

The End?

So here you are at the final stage of this journey. You have either reached these pages by diligently reading them one at a time (yes all 275) or you have decided to take a peek at the last chapter to see whether you want to start at the beginning. However you got to this page I suggest that you go back to the introduction and start again. Why? Well, most people read a book like this without stopping to do the exercises.

Self-help books are often quite inspiring. While you read you are transported into a world of possibility. Written in the words are ideas that can lift you up so you gain insight into and perspective of new and greener pastures. Your understanding of them will change with time. Inspiration and enthusiasm can fade – think of all those New Year resolutions that didn't last – that's why this book is full of exercises. It is the exercises that give you a direct and tangible, dare I say emotional experience that you can build upon. You have read about it, now go back and get into it. If you enjoyed the journey the first time round take more time now to re-experience in a different way. This time let the exercises work on you. Don't think about it. Do more than read it. Encounter it.

> *We are what we repeatedly do. Excellence then is not an act but a habit.*
>
> Aristotle

Today is the first day of the rest of your life. You are not your habits. You know your history is not your future. You can replace any patterns of self-defeating behaviour as easily as you can remember the sound of laughter or a smiling face. It would be pretty wonderful to admit to that, wouldn't it? By participating in this course you have let your standpoint slip. You have seen your perspectives alter and now you can acquire experience in a different light. You are rediscovering the diversity of your authentic self.

Rather than worship the gods of other people's opinions you can begin to live your life with a fresh and stronger sense of your own identity and integrity. Free of comparison to others, you will redefine yourself from within and find an inner directness that will guide you to fulfil your dreams and ambitions successfully.

Ironically, you will find that as you care less about what others think of you, you will notice more about how and what others think of themselves and their world – this includes their relationship with you. In lucid focus there is the opportunity to re-evaluate, repair and rebuild your relationships on solid foundations of emotional sincerity, flexibility and strength.

In candid honesty you will lose the need to pass judgement, criticize and hold opinions of how other people ought to live and behave. You will become more interested in the rediscovery and expression of your essentially unchanging deep inner essence. In an often stormy and unpredictable world this is your anchor. This is your humanity. Through it you can create your personal heaven on earth. As you find your wings I encourage you to slip 'the surly bonds of Earth'* and glide the thermals as you surf the winds of change.

Healing happens in the very moment you remember that, whatever you are. Wherever you come from. Whatever injury you have suffered or imposed on others. Whatever may have happened that has impaired your ability to give and receive love. You are the greatest power in your life and you can make it right by living every moment from this point on seeking to give and receive value, understanding, respect and love.

• What would it be like to show value and have value?

*from poem, *High Flight*, by John Gillespie Magee Jr.

- What would it be like to have respect and to give respect?
- What would it be like to be loved and be loving?
- What would it be like to be fearless instead of fearful?

I wonder, are these rhetorical questions or is this an instruction to get out those pens and paper once more and make an Emotional Map? At this point in the proceedings you know that you have a mind (and dare I say heart) of your own. It knows how to ask good quality questions and make decisions for your highest good. So, it's over to you.

Bon Voyage.

> *Oh! I have slipped the surly bonds of Earth*
> *And danced the skies on laughter-silvered wings;*
> *Sunward I've climbed, and joined the tumbling mirth*
> *Of sun-split clouds, – and done a hundred things*
> *You have not dreamed of – wheeled and soared and swung*
> *High in the sunlit silence. Hov'ring there,*
> *I've chased the shouting wind along, and flung*
> *My eager craft through footless halls of air . . .*
>
> *Up, up the long delirious, burning blue*
> *I've topped the wind-swept heights with easy grace*
> *Where never lark or ever eagle flew –*
> *And, while with silent lifting mind I've trod*
> *The high untrespassed sanctity of space,*
> *Put out my hand and touched the face of God.*

'High Flight' by Pilot Officer John Gillespie Magee Jr. – 412 Squadron RCAF, killed 11 December 1941

Index

A to Zen Youth Foundation

The A to Zen Youth Foundation is an Unincorporated Voluntary Organization (a non-profit organization) formed to bring together caring professionals who are committed to reaching out to and assisting groups of young people whose needs are often neglected by society.

The A to Zen Youth Foundation aims specifically to target children (particularly those with special needs), unmarried mothers, young adults leaving local authority residential care and adolescents serving custodial sentences.

Our objective is to inspire and motivate young people to live up to their true potential, to take care of themselves effectively and to feel willing and able to contribute to the community in which they live, and to society as a whole. With this in mind, the foundation will work tirelessly to address youth unemployment and homelessness.

It is our vision to design and supply outstanding resources for education, training and self-development through which we intend to make a substantial difference to the quality of life of these aforementioned important members of society.

A Vision In The Making
In the long term we want to change the quality of life in our country. To do so we clearly have to affect the values and beliefs of a large number of people. Our future lies in the hands of our children. And it is the personal values and expectations of these

children that will influence our own lives in the coming years. Through schemes like those funded and run by The Prince's Trust (UK) and the National and Community Service Act (1990 USA), to name but a couple, young people will contribute their time and energy to the aged, infirm, disadvantaged, the less abled and to the environment. They will invest their time, enthusiasm and energy to a larger cause and in the process will dynamically develop their identities and positively influence their future.

The power of such programmes is that they allow individuals to go beyond themselves and experience first-hand the effect of their generosity upon another human being. If one person acting unselfishly, offering practical help and kindness, can make such a difference, what would be the result should each one of us invest a part of ourselves in society as a whole? We want to give more people the opportunity to find out as they give and receive in this way.

You Can Make A Difference
Now that you have worked with the elements of the Emotional Excellence Course you will find that you spend less time worrying. You will experience more motivation and respond to life's challenges more readily. You will also have more energy to invest in your future and those that you care about. I am going to ask you to invest some of your reclaimed energy into a worthwhile cause or project of your choice. You should con-tribute only what you can comfortably afford either in time, emotional support or money. If each one of us donated just half a day a year (delivering food parcels to the needy at Christmas for instance) or the price of a pair of cinema tickets, your community and the world as a whole would be a much richer place.

Your Investment
In the short term, the A to Zen Youth Foundation wants to donate copies of this book and run heavily subsidized courses to

every homeless shelter, local authority care home, youth custodial center, and mother and baby hostel. This is our vision and we need your help to train facilitators and coach volunteers who have already committed to the A to Zen vision.

Through the Foundation, your time, energy and financial contribution will make a significant difference. We invite you to join us now and invest in helping those less fortunate than yourself.

To give your support and for more information about the Foundation please write to:

A to Zen Foundation
c/o Maya Phillips
14 Lindeth Close,
Stanmore, Middx
HA7 2RQ UK
e.mail **motex@geocities.com**

A to Zen Youth Foundation is an Unincorporated Voluntary Organization currently applying for tax exempt charity status. Until such status is obtained contributions to the Foundation will not qualify for tax exemption.